Knock Out Fear in the First Round

IbbiLane Press

copyright ©2016

ISBN-13: 978-0692772683 (IbbiLane Press)

ISBN-10: 0692772685

Table of Contents

Forward   v

Dedication   vii

Rd 1 Truth be told I'm not supposed to be here   9

Rd 2 The Bully can be beat!   31

Rd 3 Fearless is bullshit!   43

Rd 4 This Ain't Batman and Robin   55

Rd 5 The "How" don't matter   65

Rd 6 Pack it in if you won't do this   77

Rd 7 The Game Changer   93

Rd 8 You can't outperform it   105

Rd 9 The Bully Buster   121

Rd 10 The New Undisputed Champ!   133

Rd 11 Real, Raw and Live!   149

Forward

So who is Dave Daley the Monster Motivator? That was the question I asked when several people contacted me through social media telling me I had to check this guy out. What I discovered is first and foremost Dave Daley is a serial entrepreneur. A near fatal motorcycle accident proved to be the catalyst he needed to delve into personal development and his own immense potential. He's grown and sold businesses in different industries and continues to own and grow his most recent one. That would be enough of a story but there is so much more to him.

He's also a dynamic motivational speaker who is very transparent about his background, his high school dropout status and the fact he was told not to expect much from himself as an adult. Dave is known as a straight-talking authority on leadership, personal development and helping people conquer their fears so they can move forward in their lives.

Dave is one of the most passionate hosts of any type of show I've ever seen and not only puts guests of Monster Motivator TV at ease but really gets them to open up and become almost as transparent as he himself is. Many people who have been guests on his show have said they have been somehow changed simply by being around him. His enthusiasm for business and really for life itself is positively contagious. The fact that he truly cares about each and every person he comes into contact with comes through loud and clear.

For someone who was once told not to expect much at all from himself as an adult Dave has truly experienced success in its truest form...he has helped countless people conquer their fears, achieve their dreams and pay it forward by helping others themselves.

~Kellie Fitzgerald

Dedication

I am dedicating this book to multiple people for multiple reasons.

First and foremost I dedicate this book to LIFE....If it wasn't for Life's Bootcamps over the years....I wouldn't be where I am or Who I am today!

Also the people over the years that said or thought I wouldn't create anything substantial in my life....A HUGE THANK YOU! You became my propeller not my anchor. :-)

To my marketing manager Caitlin Leshiner....without her there is no Monster Motivator! TRUTH! Her drive determination dedication and loyalty to me is absolutely amazing and humbling at the same time! Caitlin is a very big part of my WHY! She is Family.

Kellie Fitzgerald my publisher and friend....Kellie gave me the opportunity to make this book a reality....She completely enhanced my weaknesses and allowed Dave Daley The Monster Motivator to stay REAL & RAW! Thank you Girl! :-)

Cyndi Lemke. Cyndi and I just started working together....But it has been a powerful connection from day one! I am so looking forward to Cyndi staying on Team DDMM...and growing with us for a long time to come!

George Elias, Big G...Thank you for all your hard work and dedication to the videos and action pics...and for makin' things happen when we need them!

Cy Rathbun. Cy, thank you for the awesome photo shoot and for being a great friend!

A HUGE "THANK YOU" TO TOMMY!

And I want to thank everyone that I have met in person and on social media that have supported us on this awesome journey....I 'm looking forward to meeting everyone as we launch MMTV nationwide!

Monster Motivator Mania Tour Coming To A Town Near You!

Sincerely,

Dave Daley

The Monster Motivator

ROUND 1

TRUTH BE TOLD...I'M NOT SUPPOSED TO BE HERE.

THE START ISN'T NEARLY AS
IMPORTANT AS THE FINISH.

The Start is not nearly as important as the Finish!

I was told I wasn't supposed to win. My early years were nothing close to successful. I was left back in the second grade and diagnosed with ADD. They told me I had a learning disorder and I never even graduated from High School.

And if that wasn't enough to start my adult life in a funk....At nineteen I'm sitting in a jail cell looking at 8-10 years if things don't go my way. Sometimes in life it's better to be lucky than good! LOL

I was told growing up in school that I wasn't supposed to win, you know, that I wasn't supposed to win in life because I couldn't learn in that classroom environment. It was just so hard for me to focus and learn in that atmosphere.

I wanted to be outside doing things that were physical like playing sports you know just releasing all that energy. That's where my comfort zone was. But you put me in that cookie-cutter classroom and it was tough! Trust me when I tell you my mother was probably in the principal's office as much as I was. Wow those early years. So again, growing up my conditioning was "I'm not supposed to win" and "don't expect a lot out of myself when I become an adult."

Like I said, I didn't even graduate High School. My senior year I was told I would have to go back to summer school again for the fourth time. I'd gone to summer school every single year and now for the fourth time in High School I was going to have to go back in order to get even close to having enough credits to graduate. I remember I said this isn't for me. I did my time and I'm ready to move on and see what else is out there. That really was my mindset.

I remember I just recently did a podcast and my guest asked me a question that no one had ever asked me before, "How did it make you feel when you walked out of High School and you just left? You said this is it and I'm done and you moved on?"

I told him I'd never really thought about it but now thinking back really the best way I can describe it is it felt like a weight lifting off my shoulders. Like an anchor lifted off my shoulders. I felt free. I was finally out of a place I felt like I didn't belong in to begin with. School for me had always been more hanging out with my friends and having a good time, playing sports and getting in trouble. That's what school was for me. That's what I looked forward to. But again, that classroom, wow that classroom environment was tough!

Now, there were three classrooms I did ace: gym, recess and lunch. Those were my favorite classes and I had no problem acing those classes! You know looking back it was a struggle, but it was a real relief when I walked out of High School. When I went home and told my parents the news, it wasn't the easiest thing to do by any means. It was tough. But I remember my dad saying "ok, well if that's the decision you've made here's what you need to do. You need to figure out what you're going to do, how you're going to support yourself, and what are you going to do to make a living."

My old conditioning went right back to what I knew and who I was and I was a physical guy so I went into construction. When I say construction I mean I did everything under the sun with construction, roofing, framing, brick work, rock work. I was in the Iron Workers union, the Laborers union, Roofers Union. Really, if it was physical, count me in!

I was kinda like the elephant in the circus. The way they train baby elephants to stay in one spot is they take a rope and tie it around his back leg and they put a stake in the ground. Every time that baby elephant tries to walk away the rope and the stake stops it. When that baby elephant becomes a grown adult it could easily pull up the stake, but when it feels the tension of the rope it stops pulling. That's conditioning. The elephant has been conditioned its whole life that it can't walk any farther than the rope so it doesn't try; even though as an adult it could easily pull up the stake and go wherever it wants whenever it wants. I was that elephant.

I grew up in a normal household. We certainly weren't rich, but we certainly weren't poor either. And I had an older brother and sister and they just cruised through school. I mean, all A's and B's and they didn't even look back. If they got a C it was total devastation in the house, "A C? How did you get a C?" I was all D's and F's if I brought home a C it was a celebration! I mean they brought the cake and candles out for the C because it was just so rare for me to get a C.

When I was in construction I rented a room from a buddy's mom and I was looking for work. There was a time when the country went through a major, major recession kinda like a depression, sort of like we did in 2007 - 2008. I was looking for work, and I was going from jobsite to jobsite and nothing was going on. Jobsites were being shut down because money wasn't moving, banks weren't lending. Back then, before the internet, you had to get the newspaper to look at the help wanted ads. So there I am on a Monday morning in the kitchen looking through the help wanted ads.

I'm going through the help wanted ads and on page 1 there is nothing, page 2 nothing, page 3 nothing. I'm thinking there's got to be something right, I need work, and I need to pay bills. I've got no money, no job, bills right around the corner. I have to eat, pay bills and survive. So I go back to page 1 thinking maybe I missed something. Scanning page 1 and all of a sudden

I see this ad and it just jumps right out at me. It says, "Outside sales, selling copiers and fax machines B to B."

I thought, man I don't know anything about outside sales. At that time it wasn't even on my radar. I mean, selling copiers and fax machines? I know what they are, but I certainly don't know enough about them to sell them. And "B to B" I don't even know what that means at the time. But under that in big, bold letters was "No experience necessary, will train." I thought you don't have to look any farther, that's my resume they're talking about...I have no experience and I need somebody to train me in something. Right underneath that it says "please call to set up an interview."

An interview? OK, so I figure how hard can this be? I'm in the kitchen and I pick up the phone and dial the number. The phone rings. "Hi welcome to Heritage business Systems, how can we help you?" Click. I mean I was like a deer in headlights. I couldn't talk. I mean that bubbly voice just threw me off and I had no idea what to say. So there I am in the kitchen, I'm pacing, palms are sweating, my heart is pumping...what am I going to do? I've got to be able to talk, I've got to be able to pick up the phone and make the appointment to have any shot at this. So I'm pacing back and forth and a few more minutes go by and I'm looking at the phone. The only thing keeping me there are those big bold letters "No Experience Necessary, Will Train." That and I have no job, no money and bills are right around the corner.

So, I pick up that phone, oh how I did not want to make that call, but I dialed that number, phone rings. "Hi, welcome to Heritage Business systems, how can we help you?" Um, hi my name's Dave and I'm calling about the ad in the paper. "Oh for the outside sales job?" Um, yeah. "Oh when would you like to come in?" Um, well, I can come in tomorrow. "Oh great, we have a 9:00 will that work?" Thank God she was helping me, right? I said sure, that will be fine. She said, "Ok great, if you have a pen and paper I will give you our address and we'll see you tomorrow at 9." So I write down the address and she says "Great, have a great day and we'll see you tomorrow!" Click.

I'm thinking, have a great day? Have a great day? I mean I did it but I'm thinking what did I do? Now I have a professional interview and I have no idea what to do, what to say, what to expect... Now fast forward the clock and it's dinner time and we're sitting down, we're eating dinner and I say to my buddy's mom "Kat I have this professional interview tomorrow for an outside sales job." She says "you do? that's great." She's always been really supportive. But I say "I know, but I don't know what to say, I don't know what to do, I don't think I should go." She said "you're going to be fine. Just make sure you look professional, make sure you wear a suit and tie because your first impression is everything."

So, OK, I get done with dinner and I go upstairs and I've got one suit and tie, right, and it had seen its better days a long time ago. You're not seeing this one in Nordstrom's any time soon. I mean it had been through weddings, funerals and court, that's what I had this suit for. So I get this suit out and make sure it's not wrinkled. Morning comes and I put this suit on and make sure I look OK, I look down and the tie looks OK, shoes look alright and out the door I go.

I start heading to the interview, I pull into the parking lot and there is a lineup of cars. Mercedes, BMWs, Audis, Jaguars...here I come in my CJ5 brown rusted out Jeep. I pull in and go way over to the right hoping nobody sees me and I get out and start walking up to the entrance. And it is a huge white stucco building, huge letters "Heritage Business Systems" I mean this thing could have been the Taj Mahal and it would have been no different to me.

So I walk in and head to the receptionist "Hi welcome to Heritage Business systems..." It's that voice. I say hi, um, I'm um, Dave, she says "OH you're the 9:00" Yes, I am. "Here, take this paperwork and grab a seat in the lobby and Mike the General Manager will be with you shortly."

So I'm in the lobby, and I'm filling out the paperwork and looking around. There are sale people going in and out, the girls in the front are taking messages and answering calls and I'm sitting in this lobby. I'm thinking gee, everyone around here looks like they know exactly what they're doing, they look so professional. And I'm saying to myself they look so damn smart right, and I'm just a laborer, what am I doing here? I'm trying to fill this paperwork out and I'm looking around and I keep looking at that door. I mean, I'm ready to make a run for it any second now. But I keep filling paperwork out, looking around and looking at the door.

"Hi are you Dave?" Yeah, hi, I'm Dave. "Hi, I'm Mike the General Manager." Very nice to meet you. "Just come on back and we'll get the interview started." So we go back to his office and we walk in. There's a big beautiful wrap-around desk, big leather chair, gold-plated pens, everything in perfect order. He says "grab a seat." I sit down, he sits down and he leans back in that big leather chair and he's looking at my information.

So he's asking me questions and we're going back and forth for, I don't know, about 15 minutes or so and I'm answering in the best way that I can and in the most professional way I know of at the time. All of a sudden he stands up and he walks toward the door. He says "I'll be right back" then walks out and closes the door behind him.

Here I am in this big office. I have no idea, is this good, is this bad? I've never been in this position before in my life but all I know is my old conditioning comes right back and there I am back in grade school, middle school, and my mom's going to come into the principal's office and they're going to start yelling and screaming at me because I did something wrong somehow, someway, right?

So I'm sitting in this big office looking around and I don't want to touch anything, I don't want to break anything and I'm just sitting there looking around and the door opens. Here comes Mike and right behind him, this short stocky burly guy. This guy's wearing a beautiful Italian suit, black with a grey pinstripe and a hanky that matches. Mike says "I'd like to introduce you to Tom. Tom is the owner of the company." I said, Tom it's a pleasure to meet you.

Now Tommy, Tommy wasn't big on words but he was huge on impact, you know, one of those types of people. To give you a little visual on Tommy, he was a combination of Joe Pesci and Danny Devito. Now, Mike goes and sits down and Tommy says "grab a seat, kid." So, I sit down. Now, Tommy doesn't sit, he's just leaning against the wall and he's got my information in front of him. He's just looking at my paperwork, looking at Mike, looking at me. Finally he looks down and says "looks like all you've done is construction. Looks like you don't have any experience in outside sales." I said no, to be honest with you Tommy, I've never done any kind of outside sales, I've just been a laborer.

Tommy keeps looking at the paperwork, looking at Mike, looking at me, looks back down at the paperwork and says to me "what makes you think you even want to try this? What makes you think you can even do this?" I said, Tommy, you know I saw your ad in the paper and it said no experience necessary and that you would train and I thought I could give it a shot. There's no work out there in construction. Tommy's still looking down at the paperwork, looking at Mike, looking at me, looks back down at the paperwork.

17

Finally he says "Alright" and walks over to Mike and hands him the clipboard, then leans over and shakes my hand. Then he says "it was very nice to meet you." I said "Oh, Tommy it was a pleasure to meet you." He starts walking to the door, turns around and says "meet me here at 5 o'clock tonight." Then he walks out and closes the door behind him. I'm looking at Mike, thinking what just happened. Mike starts wrapping up the interview then walks me out and says to make sure I get there a little early to meet Tommy tonight.

I'm driving home and thinking why am I going to meet him at 5? Why 5? I don't understand. They'll be closed. But, ten minutes until 5 there I am in the lobby and here comes Tommy briefcase in hand saying "come on kid, follow me." We walk out and get into his car, a big beautiful black Mercedes with leather interior. We start driving, Tommy's making small talk and I have no idea what's going on. What are we doing? Where are we going? To be honest with you, I'm just a little afraid to ask. I mean, I'm a kid from Jersey; Tommy could be in a whole different line of business than selling copiers and fax machines.

So we're driving and after about ten minutes we pull into this parking lot of a retail outlet store. We park and Tommy says "come on kid" and we start walking up to the entrance. We walk in and there's a salesman right over to the left of the entrance. "Hey guys, welcome to Sam's! Anything I can do to help you, please let me know." Tommy goes, "I need three shirts, three ties, three suits for this kid." The salesman looks at Tommy then looks at me. I look at Tommy then at the salesman. I have no idea what's going on. The salesman says "Yeah, yeah, come on back to the men's department." He sure didn't want to lose this sale!

We start following him back to the men's department and I look back at Tommy. He's completely straight-faced, not showing anything at all. You don't want to play poker with Tommy,

18

you'd never know if this guy's holding Jokers or Aces, right. We keep walking back and we get to the men's department and all of a sudden I've got shirts coming at me, ties coming at me they're measuring me for suits. Now the salesman's got three shirts, three ties, three suits and they all match beautifully.

The salesman starts writing up the ticket and hands it to Tommy and tells him the suits will be done in a few days. Tommy gives him his card and says "Just let me know." He grabs the ticket, walks up and pays the girl at the cash register, gets the receipt and says "come on kid." We walk out of the store and get into his car.

I tell Tommy I can't pay him for these suits. I don't have any money, I'm broke. Tommy laughed "Don't worry about it kid, 'cause you're going to pay me back with the commissions you earn." Tommy had a sort of demented sense of humor; he liked to see people squirm. I figured I must be hired. So he drops me off at my truck and tells me to meet him here at 8 o'clock tomorrow morning and be ready to work. You're going to work directly with me. I going to teach you exactly what we do and how we do it.

OK. So I'm driving home and I'm thinking that at least I'm hired, right. At ten before 8 there I am in the lobby and here comes Tommy wearing another beautiful suit. "Come on kid, follow me." We get into his car and start driving. Tommy asks "do you know anything about cold calling?" I had no idea, so I told him I'd never even heard of it. He told me to just watch what he did, listen and learn and that he would do all the talking. I thought that was really good, because if I did any talking it wasn't going to go well because I had no idea what I was doing.

Now when you're an outside sales rep for Tommy's company you're required to do 40 to 50 cold calls a day, five days a week. They were grooming me to be an outside sales rep for them in center city Philly. So we're working together for about a week and a half and Tommy's taking the lead on everything and I'm just following and listening, trying to learn everything. In between businesses he would coach me. About a week and a half in we go into the city one morning and we walk up to this big, 45-story building. I mean a beautiful glass-mirrored building. Tommy said we're going to work that building today. When you work the high-rises in the city, you start on the top floor and work your way down.

We get into the elevator and go all the way to the 45th floor. Now at this time there was an attorney's office that was so big it occupied the top three floors of this building and their headquarters was on the 45th floor - the penthouse. The elevator door opens at the 45th floor, we get out, make a left and go down this little hallway and make a quick right and there's the entrance to this attorney's firm. I never had seen anything like it. It looked like a movie set. There was Italian marble on the floors, artwork wrapped around the walls, a wrap around aquarium and a waterfall in the entrance to this attorney's firm. Plus they were so big they had four girls right out front as receptionists. I mean these girls were busy! They were taking messages and routing calls like phone operators.

So we start walking into the entrance and we start heading toward the center girl. I'm sort of looking around this place, just looking around, thinking where in the world are we. We make our way up to the receptionist and I'm still just in awe, just looking around. "Hi, can I help you?" asked the receptionist. I look around and Tommy's gone. "Hi, can I help you please?" she questions again. I'm stammering, um, hi, yeah, I, I, I, um. Then I hand her my card and tell her I'm Dave from Heritage Business Services. She says "this is the gentleman you need to speak to" and takes my card and gives me the other card and gets right back on the phone. So, I've got this card in my hand

and I'm turning around and I mean, I want to run but they're all looking at me. My heart's pumping out of my chest.

I've got this card and I'm walking and I'm wondering where did Tommy go? Now I see Tommy, he's out in the hallway leaning on the wall next to the elevator. I say "Tommy, what happened, where were you? Look, I got the decision maker, I got the card." Tommy looks down at the card, looks at me and laughs "I knew you could do it kid." There I am. I've got the card in my hand. I did it. From that point on, and we worked together for about another week or so, I took the lead on every job. Then Tommy would coach me.

You know, I share this story and I get involved in this story because there are a lot of points in this story. Obviously it changed the whole direction of my life. Tommy was a really amazing mentor and he never really realized it. In fact, if I talked to Tommy today and told him he was my first mentor he'd look at me like I was crazy. That's just who Tommy was. When you look back at this story, there's a reason things happen and I share this in my keynotes. I'm a big believer in the why and the fact that things always happen with the same recipe, just different ingredients. I say that all the time.

Again, what happened in this story changed the whole direction of my life. It got me out of construction and made me realize I could do other things. You have to understand, when I came to the interview, when I answered that ad, I on paper had no business being in that place. I had no experience in that industry. No experience in outside sales. I was just a laborer up until that time in my life. But Tommy saw something in me. He took a chance. I always say if your "why" is big enough it's going to pull you through those fear barriers. When your "why" becomes bigger than you...you become unstoppable.

You need to understand at that time in my life Tommy was the first successful adult that told me they believed in me. And he showed me that he believed in me the minute that he bought me three suits within 12 hours of meeting me. He invested in me from day one. So there's nothing I wouldn't do for Tommy. I'd walk through fire for Tommy at that time. My "why" had just become bigger than me and there's no way I'd let him down. I became an outside sales rep for Tommy's company and I know people have wondered, you know, did Tommy ever get his money back for those suits? Well, let me tell you, Tommy got his money back and then some. Tommy knew exactly what he was doing and Tommy was no dummy!

Tommy was my first real mentor. He helped me understand there was more out there and there were a lot of things I could bring to the table. I just didn't realize it and I'd never had the opportunity. From that point on, I worked for Tommy for a while, but when I moved on I stayed in sales. And I always stayed in 100% sales commission, I always was that 100% sales commission guy because I loved the freedom. I was always self-driven and I hated to be micro-managed and that's probably why I never liked school, right? I didn't like being in that box, being in that classroom always being "micro-managed."

My personality, my DNA, has always been "just show me what needs to be done and if I believe in it, I'll run with it." So I've been doing different outside sales jobs from that point on and then my at the time best friend's dad had a public adjustment firm in New Jersey and he was looking for some outside sales guys that were going to be on straight commission. That was right up my alley, right? A public adjuster for anybody that doesn't know is a licensed adjuster that works strictly for the homeowner, the policy-holder. Public Adjusters negotiate on behalf of the homeowner or policy-holder with the insurance company to maximize their settlement.

I worked in the Public Adjustment industry for probably about 8 or 9 years, the first four with this friend's dad's company and a little over four years with another company. Then I went ahead and started up my own public adjustment firm. Now the last company that I worked for was sort of a partnership thing because I had partnered with an adjuster. I had been the sales guy then there were adjusters that would process the claims. This guy, Tommy, (I know something about that name, but not the same Tommy) he was about my age, we were both in our middle 20's, as we just both decided to leave that company and start our own.

It's interesting how things unfold. This was the first time when someone else helped pull me through my fear barriers. I was ready to make the move, pull the trigger, but I was getting nervous. I was getting cold feet. Tommy, my partner at the time, said you know what, let's just do this. So he actually pulled me through my fear barrier. From that point on once we started that business it just took off. I did all the sales, I brought in all the claims, we had an office manager who would process everything and Tommy would adjust it. For the first year and a half after we started we really starting crushing it. Things were going really well, we were working six or seven days a week, and all of a sudden Tommy just started to unravel.

Tommy just couldn't handle the pressure, and he had his own demons, drinking, drugs and gambling. Believe it or not, he had all three. He wanted out, he needed to get out. So here I am a year and a half into my first business ever and I'm sitting with attorneys and accountants trying to figure out how to buy him out, what it's worth. But I still need to run this business. I was completely and utterly out of my comfort zone. I was at a point in my life that was really, really tough. It was really hard to figure out how to keep running the business while trying to buy him out, figure out what's fair on both ends, figure out a payment plan, I mean it was like going through a divorce. But I made it through and I became stronger from it. And I learned a ton from it.

Then it was about four and a half years in and I realize that I want out. I wanted to sell. My issue was there's that fear barrier again, right, if I sell what am I going to do, this is all I know. That's what kept coming up, that's what my self-talk was. "You can't do anything else, what are you going to do, what happens from there?" I was married at that time and my wife said, "You know we're going back and forth, trying to figure this out together (she worked for me) why don't we take a long weekend and just relax, clear our minds, and we're going to figure this out." Since it was summertime, she said we should go up to her dad's vacation home in Vermont.

So we take a long weekend, we pack everything up, we've got the dogs in the truck and we head up to Vermont. We leave Jersey early Friday morning. We get up to Vermont early Friday afternoon and my brother-in-law says hey let's take a ride on the bikes. He had his buddy's bike and I could use his bike (motorcycles). So we get on the bikes and we start driving and we're going down these winding roads in Vermont. All of a sudden I hit this divot and the whole front of the bike starts to shake. Instead of me letting off the throttle and letting it ride it out I tried to wrestle through it, hit the throttle and it sent me right into a boulder. I went head-first into this boulder and my brother-in-law makes a turn and doesn't see me so he comes back and finds me literally in a tree, unconscious. He pulls me down and I come to and I can't breathe, I'm having trouble breathing.

The paramedics come and take me to the hospital. They put me in the "tube" to see if there's any internal bleeding and if there was they would have to fly me to New York because their facility couldn't handle it. Luckily there was no internal bleeding but I broke everything on my right side and punctured a lung, that's why I was having trouble breathing. I was in intensive care for a few days and I work my way up to being strong enough to get out of intensive care but I was still in the hospital. I said to my wife, I just have to get out of here. I made a deal with my doctor, he said OK, if you can walk down that hallway, up that ramp, past the nurses' desk and come back I'll sign you out. Oh man, it took me a while, but I did it. So he signed me out and I get out of the hospital. I'm back at the vacation house in Vermont for a few more days then I head back home to Jersey. I am beat up. What am I going to do?

Here's the thing, during those worst parts of your life when everything is dark, if you're willing to look, those can be the best times of your life. That day made me realize tomorrow is not guaranteed for any of us, our life can change within a minute. That gave me the courage I needed. Within the next year I wound up selling my business and starting a fire restoration business. Without that accident I honestly don't know if I would have been able to sell, especially when I did. I would have been miserable. That life lesson really made me wake up.

Here I am I started a fire restoration business with one of the adjusters I had when I had the public adjustment firm. I started that business in 2000 and had it for seven years. Things were going really good. Then in 2005 my wife and I took a ten day vacation to San Diego. From San Diego we went to Santa Monica. We ended in Santa Monica on the 10th day, we were at the hotel, we were eating breakfast and I remember looking out at the beach. I said to her "Michelle, we've got to live here. We've gotta move here, this place is absolutely amazing. I felt at home from day one."

Now we'd been together a long time and she knows me very well and she knew I had that look in my eyes. We'd had our issues as a couple and we'd been going through counseling right around that time so we'd been having our obstacles in our relationship. Between the end of 2006 and the beginning of 2007 we separated and by November 2007 the divorce had gone through. We are still close and talk at least a few times a year. When I go back east I still stay with her family, I'm still very close with my ex-in-laws. But the week of Thanksgiving, 2007, I made settlement on my house, settlement on the business and my divorce went through. So major, major changes in my life, major overhaul of my life at the end of 2007 and coming into 2008.

Now at that time I'd been coming out to San Diego for a week at a time since 2006 just to get acclimated and I just fell in love with the area every time. Every time I had to get back on that plane to go back to New Jersey I'd get so bummed out because I just loved Southern California so much. In 2008 I had about a six month window before I moved out to San Diego full time so I got all my ducks in a row and just made sure everything was good to go. So there I am, I moved out to San Diego, I'm in Point Loma, and it's July 2008. Just me and my dog. I have no idea what business I'm going to do or what I'm going to get into next, but I made a deal with myself. I said, if I'm going to make this big move, if I'm going to move across the country by myself, just me and my dog here's the deal. The deal is it has to be passion related first, profit second.

I had always looked at profit margins first and hadn't worried whether I had a passion for it or not. I started looking at personal training studios, maybe starting my own personal training studio because I had my own personal training certification back east because I'd done it part time. I loved it, but in the economy it didn't make a lot of sense. I kept moving and kept taking action and I'm a big believer that when you keep taking that consistent positive action the people and circumstances come into your life that make things happen.

Well, one of the first things that I did as soon as I moved into Point Loma was I signed up at Gold's Gym. I already knew all the guys there because when I'd go for a week at a time I always trained there. They said, oh you finally did it! You finally made the move.

So I made the move and I'm out there full time. I have the gym membership. The next thing on my list is to find a good supplement store. The guys at the gym told me about this place called "The Nutrition Zone" that just opened up and it's right across the street. I go over there and meet the owner, John. What a great guy! He's from the east coast, we really hit it off. After a few weeks, I'd been going in there all the time and we'd talk. He told me this was a new franchise and they're from the Orange County area and they might be looking for other people to open up franchises. I thought, wow, this is perfect. I had really wanted to open up a sports nutrition store back east when I had my fire restoration business but we just got so busy that it never happened.

I decided to get in touch with the owner and we talked. He told me they had a store that was already open. It had been open for about a year and it was really struggling, if you want you can take a look at it or find a new location. So, I go to this store, check it out, I see what's going on and I tell him I see some things that I think I might be able to implement that I think would really make a difference. Now, I didn't know for sure, I was still taking a chance but knock on wood with a lot of blood, sweat and tears I decided to buy the store.

On November 16, 2008 I signed everything and took the store over. Now, again I'd never been in that industry, but I'd been around that industry for such a long time and had such a passion for it. I thought you know there are things they didn't do that I think that I could do. So I started doing free seminars, I came up with several promotional opportunities for my clients, for the customers and brought as much value as I could. Within the first year and a half we actually tripled the numbers at that location in a bad economy through, again, a lot of blood, sweat and tears and we became the "go to" for sports nutrition in North County.

Now it's the middle of 2010 and coming into 2011 and one of the stipulations in the contract for franchise owners is that they wouldn't allow any franchise owner to be a part of the on-line business. It didn't take long to realize that's where everything's going, right, by the minute everything's transitioning in that industry to on-line and brick and mortar is going to be obsolete. In probably the next ten years I would say. I started to see where that trend was going and I knew the contract stopped us from getting into the on-line business. So I decided to build the equity as much as I could and flip it. That's what I did. I kept building and building and building and by the spring of 2012 I actually flipped it back to the home office, the corporation.

Now, again when you start taking action, people and circumstances, things start to unfold. At the same time that I'm looking to sell, having built equity, the owner is looking to bring partners in and he brought this big, big-time partner who rode out very successful franchises. So this guy bought in as a big-time partner with very, very deep pockets. Now that gave me someone to actually sell to who had the money to actually buy this store back. They wanted to buy the successful stores back because they'd started moving in a different direction. They weren't looking to franchise anymore, they were looking for more and more corporate stores. This new partner had enough capital to finance this and roll this out in such a big way. There was my opportunity to get out and there's their opportunity to take on a store that's now booming. It was a win-win.

I actually took about a year off and was doing some on-line businesses, but that didn't really get my juices flowing. I'm just not a behind the scenes kind of guy, I'm more out front. By 2014 I got that itch, I had to do something. So I went back to what I knew and started another fire restoration company, the company I still run at this time, June 2016. Today of course I also have a personal development business, Monster Motivator TV, and the reason that I decided to do this is because back about 17 years ago I was introduced to personal development and it changed my life. Every area of my life, personal, professional and physical was changed and it got to a point where I couldn't get enough of it. I just studied it, listened to it and had some of the greatest mentors through the years that really helped catapult me and move me forward in such a great positive direction.

Now I'm going to tell you, if it wasn't for the amount of personal development that I brought into my life my divorce would have not gone in any way the way it did. We literally split everything down the middle...my business, the house, it cost us $800 for an attorney. That's unheard of. My ex-wife is actually a testimonial on my website. You'll see her name, Michelle, and her testimonial. That's the proudest thing I've ever done in my life is to be together and married to my ex-wife for 17 years and to be able to leave that relationship the way we did and the way we still handle ourselves. I still love her, I'm just not "in love" and she feels exactly the same way. We just grew apart. That being said personal development is just a passion of mine that is so, so deep because of it's made such a difference for me in my life and I love to share it.

So why not build a business around it so I can explode this and help as many people as I can. That's where I'm at today. Monster Motivator TV is going to be in every single city in this country and we're coming soon to a city near you! The Monster Motivator tour! Keep an eye out for it by 2018 we are going to explode on the scene! I am so excited to be able to help so many people that really want the help. So that's really my story from beginning to end. It doesn't matter where you start it only matters where you end. Sometimes the only thing between you and the ride of a lifetime is you getting in the saddle and seeing what you're made of.

ROUND 2

THE BULLY CAN BE BEAT!

FEAR BARRIERS ARE BULLIES. STEP UP AND WATCH THAT BULLY DISAPPEAR!

31

In order to understand and crash through those fear barriers we really need to understand what fear is and define it so we're clear and we know how to address it and get through it. We're going to do one of two things when those fear barriers come up. We're either going to meet it head-on, break right on through, hit that fascination and not look back or we're going to let it bully us right back into safety.

Fear barriers really are bullies. See, every time it beats you it moves you down a notch. It takes away from your inner confidence and beats up your self image. You can't let a bully keep taking from you and bully you around because it keeps getting worse. The only way to stop a bully is to step up and gain that respect back. In this instance we're talking about getting your inner confidence back and getting your own inner self-respect back which comes down to your own self image.

So, "fear barriers," what are they? Fear barriers are really just obstacles created inside of our own minds. We make them up inside our own heads. It really becomes an illusion when you break through a fear barrier and realize there's nothing there, the fear disappears. In this book I'm going to show you that there are really layers to fear. It isn't just about facing your fears and they'll disappear, there are actually layers to this formula that will help you identify and crush through those fear barriers. I'm going to share that with you throughout this book.

Right now let's get into fear barriers and why they appear. There are really numerous reasons fear barriers appear depending on the person and the circumstance. One example is the fear of the unknown. You know, finding yourself in that uncharted territory, finding yourself in that darkness. Or finding yourself outside of your comfort zone or those fears of "what if" like what if this happens or what if that happens. The fear of failure is a big one, "if I do this and I fail, then what?" Then there's the fear of other people and of what other people think and that fear of failing in front of people and fearing what they'll think about your failure. This one is a big, big fear barrier for a lot of people; they just don't understand it, they don't know the definition of it and it stops them every single time.

There is also the fear of success. What does the fear of success really look like? The fear of success is really the fear of new responsibility, taking on that new responsibility or that new title or position. It could also be starting or taking over a new business. The fear of success also ties in with the fear of "who do I need to become." Like, if I need to become this new person to take on this level of success are my old friends and those people in my life going to still accept me? What happens is that people get so caught up in all of this they lose focus on what they really want to do. Ultimately it all comes back to the fear of success. It will stop you every single time if you don't know how to stop it, address it and move forward.

This is a huge fear for anyone in business. If you're a leader and you don't know how to conquer this fear you won't thrive or even survive in business. This fear is the fear of change. The most toxic statement you can hear in business is "we've been doing this forever." Or "we've always done it this way and we're going to continue to do it this way." The reason those are such toxic statements is because they're saying they're not willing to grow, expand or move forward. If you aren't sure how accurate that statement is, just ask Blockbuster video, Borders books or Kodak film.

It doesn't matter how big you are or how long you've been in business, if you can't identify that fear barrier of change and learn how to crush right through it for you and your organization you're going to become obsolete. We're always doing one of two things, we're either moving forward or we're moving backwards. When we move backwards long enough, we disappear. In the world we live in today, it is vital to learn how to understand and handle the fear of change every single time it shows its face because we are living in a time like no other. We are evolving and changing by the second. The technology in the life we're living today is just unparalleled.

I remember about a year ago I had a cell phone that was about a year old. I went into the Barns & Noble because I was looking for a protective case for it. I walk in and go over to where the cell phones are and there are two or three young kids working there. I asked them if they could help me for a second, I was looking for a case for my phone. So the kid comes over and looks at my phone, he grabs the phone out of my hand and walks over to the other two people working there. They were all looking at my phone and kind of giggling. He finally comes back and tells me they don't have a case for that phone. I said "you don't have a case for this phone? It's an I-phone." He looked at me and said "yeah, but it's old." I told him it was only a year old but to him it was an old phone. These kids got a big laugh out of telling me my phone was old. It was only a year old but that's how fast technology is changing, how fast things are moving for us today.

So if you can't identify the changes and stay on the cutting edge of your industry you are going to be obsolete. You're going to be gone because you're not going to be bringing enough value.

There are so many different fears that people have that are stopping them. Listen, if you're a CEO, a business owner, a manager, a general manager, sales manager, office manager, a mom, a dad, an older sibling...you are a leader. In one way or other you are a leader, there are people who are looking to you to lead them. If you don't have or aren't any of those, if you work for a company and have no responsibility or if you have no family, you still need to lead your own life. So no matter what, you still need to learn how to identify and crush through those dreaded fear barriers on a consistent basis or you're going to be pretty much obsolete. You aren't going to have enough value in life.

When you don't have enough value in life people don't want to be around you, people don't want to pay you, and people will think you offer nothing. All because you didn't crush through the fear, the biggest thing that stops people is the fear. Whatever your fear is.

A lot of time it's just the fear of the unknown. When you start moving toward that unknown you start to move into the darkness because of the uncertainty. But understand, as you keep moving and as you keep taking action the darkness will only be temporary. You just have to keep moving. But if you stop and go backward into safety you're letting that fear bully win. You're letting that bully take your lunch money. And what's going to happen? If you let that bully take your lunch money today what do you think is going to happen tomorrow? That bully is going to come and take your lunch money again, and again, and again until you stop and step up to that bully.

When you step up to a bully one of two things happens. You either get knocked down or you break right through. Either way you win because you've built your self-image back up, you know you can take this head-on. Even if you fall down that fear barrier is gone because you've faced it and it's just an illusion.

The first chapter in this book is really all about fears because it stops us every single time if we allow it to. My very first business that I started I had a business partner who actually pulled me through my fear barriers even though I didn't realize it at the time. I'd never had a business before, I'd been an outside sales rep for a long time with straight commission but when I decided to go into business with a partner I actually got cold feet. He pulled me through. But once he pulled me through I realized my fear barrier was just an illusion. From that point on, fear never stopped me from making decisions and moving forward. There are always going to be things in your life that are going to happen that will help pull you through, help you identify and crush through those fear barriers. A lot of the time you won't realize it at the time but when you look back and analyze what happened - that's exactly what happened.

I can give you numerous stories. I had a really bad, nearly fatal, motorcycle accident right at the time I was deciding whether or not I was going to sell my first business. I'd had that fear of "well this is all I know, what else can I do?" That near-fatal motorcycle accident really woke me up and made me realize, you know, life just smacked me in the face and said "you don't know-there might not be a tomorrow." Tomorrow is not guaranteed for any of us. Once I recovered I realized that accident helped me make a decisive decision to sell my business. Within that year I'd actually sold the business and moved on. By identifying and breaking through that fear barrier I never had it inhibit me again when I was ready to make decisions. I learned that if it felt right I made the decision and moved forward.

I fell down, got back up. I fell down again, got back up. Fell down again, got back up. But I wouldn't allow that fear barrier to block me or stop me anymore. The reason I was able to do that and I still can today in those decision-making circumstances is because I'd already faced it. I learned that it is not life and death. I survived. So that builds my inner confidence, it builds my self image so I can take on more. Take on more chances, take more risk because tomorrow is not guaranteed and today is all we have. At the end of the day, we have this one life that we know of, one bite of the apple and that really put things into perspective instantly for me regarding fear and fear barriers. I decided there were other things I could learn and other opportunities.

I also had to realize that for me, well I needed that change. My inner self was talking to me telling me I needed a change. I was bored the business wasn't giving me anything back anymore except for monetarily. But I had to find that courage to move forward, right? Once I did, I never looked back. I've built and sold three businesses in three different industries over the past 20 years all because initially I was able to break through that fear.

That's why I'm writing this book. At the end of the day we're all confronted by fear. Now, we can let fear stop us and bully us back into safety and we'll start moving backwards until we ultimately disappear or we can let that fear ignite us, light a fire under us and allow us to thrive. That controlled energy that controlled fear can be an incredible motivation. When you tie that in with your "why," your inspiration, you really do become unstoppable.

It's really all about how we look at it, what our perspective is, and how we're willing to address it. Fear can be your best friend or it can be your worst nightmare. That is up to you, that's your decision. But you're not going to be able to do anything until you learn how to identify your fear and learn how to crush through those fear barriers. That is truly what this book is all about.

Fear barriers relate to every single person in this world no matter where they are or where they intend on going in their life. Everything is so completely based on fear. Only you can decide whether fear becomes your best friend or your worst enemy. Remember back to when you first started learning to drive, or learning to drive a stick shift, and all those fears. How am I going to steer, how to push the clutch and/or how to shift gears. How am I going to do all of those things and still watch the road? Remember how all that anxiety and fear started to build up the first few times you got behind the wheel? Now, if you've driven for any length of time it's second nature. You crushed that fear barrier. You dominated that fear barrier. That's really the key, to learn how to dominate your fears. The only way to do it is just to do it.

You're not going to be able to break through fear barriers in a classroom. You're not going to be able to break through fear barriers by reading a book. There will be steps to help you identify and learn some techniques to use to crush through those fear barriers like those I'll share with you in this book. But the book alone is not going to do it for you. A classroom alone is not going to do it. Your teacher is not going to do it, your parents are not going to do it coaches are not going to do it. The only way to really crush through fear barriers is to actually do it yourself.

A lot of times that's where people fall down. They think other people can do it for them. For example, my partner in my first business didn't really break through my fear barrier for me he just shared some thoughts with me that made me look at things in a different way. That helped me break through my fear barriers myself. Looking back there was sort of a sense of security too because I had someone else in that business with me. Maybe I wouldn't have done it if I was by myself at the time, in fact there's a good chance I might not have.

Ultimately I still had to take those steps myself. I still had to navigate through that darkness of fear. I had to do that. The other thing that happens when you start to have those fear barriers is they start feeling like they're overwhelming. The kryptonite for fear is always action. When you start taking action in a positive and consistent way it starts diminishing the fears. The reason most people don't take that action is their fear of what the outcome could be or what the "big green hairy monster" might really look like.

I wrote an e-book a while back called "The Monster Under the Bed." The premise of this book is you're ten years old and you're in your room. The lights are out and it's pitch dark. You're under the covers and you hear this sound and you're just staring at the ceiling. You know for sure there's a big green hairy monster and it's about to come out and eat you. We've all been there. Until an adult comes in, turns on the light and you look under the bed and there's no monster.

It's the exact same thing that happens when we become adults. We find ourselves in uncharted territory, we find ourselves in this darkness and we create our own big green hairy monsters. We have two choices, we can meet that big green hairy monster head on, beat that bully and not look back and meet our destination or we can let it bully us right back in to safety and stop moving forward. We always have that choice. But there is more to it than simply facing your fears and they'll disappear, that's just a part of the equation.

I'll be sharing all of this throughout this book, so stay with me and I promise you that everything I'll share are real life practical steps brought to you through my real life practical results. Each step will be very, very simple not always easy but very "apply-able." Every single thing I share I've done throughout the years and mentors I've had have done through the years. We call that combined wisdom. There's a difference between "knowledge" and "wisdom" and it's that wisdom comes from real life experiences. That wisdom is the only way we're able to conquer our fears.

Look at anything you've done in your life, at the very beginning it's so scary, but after a while when you start to dominate and master it whatever it is it becomes second nature. It's all part of your journey. When you look at fear barriers as being a part of your whole journey you start to change your perspective. You start to embrace fear because it's all part of your adventure. If you don't want any adventure in this life you were given you've got to ask yourself why you're here. This is your one life (that we're aware of) and it goes by so fast. If you live a full life, 80 or 90 years old, it's going to go by so quick you can't believe it. If you leave this world with regrets just because of some sort of thought that created fear in your mind that stopped you from doing something you really wanted to do, that's on you.

At the end of the day life is pretty simple it gives you what you earn. If you're not willing to learn how to identify and crush through those fear barriers then you haven't earned it and you really don't deserve it and you don't want it that bad. When you turn that around and you learn how to identify those fear barriers and crush through them you will earn it and whatever you really want will come to you and you will build from there. You'll keep building and create that self image where you feel unstoppable. That doesn't mean you won't make mistakes, you'll just feel unstoppable so you'll keep moving forward. It's much easier to get back up when you do make mistakes when you feel unstoppable because you've built a strong self image by breaking through fear barriers.

You learn that if you fall down you learn from it and move forward. You learn that when you fall down you either learn something or you win. When you take on that mindset you become "bullet proof" you become truly unstoppable. I want to make sure I make this clear for you. At the end of the day, fear barriers are just an illusion.

There is a difference between fear and danger. Danger is real. If you go to the top of a 20 story building and you go to the edge and look down that's danger because you could fall and die. But fear is an illusion that's built up in our minds that becomes that big green hairy monster that we can defeat by identifying and crushing right through it.

Hopefully this chapter has helped you and there are some things in it that you will begin to implement. Ultimately I hope this chapter will help you start to change and shift your conditioning, that paradigm, and you'll start looking at fear barriers as a good thing rather than as a bad thing. If you don't have fear barriers coming at you consistently you're not growing and you're not evolving. After a while, what happens? You're going to disappear, there's just not going to be any value in your life. As you start to move forward your fear barriers are going to get stronger, they're going to get bigger and they're going to get scarier. But if you're doing what you're supposed to be doing, you're going to get bigger, stronger and more able to handle whatever fears come up. To paraphrase Bruce Lee here, don't wish for things to be easier, wish for you to be stronger. That's exactly what this chapter has been all about. Focus on what you want rather than what you don't want and when you do, things start to fall into place.

Again, it all comes down to your self-image, you can build it up or tear it down but you can't ever outperform it. The only way to build it up is to break through fear barriers and build that inner confidence, move forward and take chances. The way you tear it down is to let that fear barrier bully you back into safety, not move forward or take chances. Whether you realize it or not you take chances every day just by living. Stay with me and in this book I'll give you tools you can use to crush through any fear barrier you encounter for the rest of your life.

ROUND 3

FEARLESS IS BULLSHIT!

THE DARKNESS IS ONLY TEMPORARY IF YOU KEEP MOVING FORWARD. IT BECOMES PERMANENT WHEN YOU MOVE BACK INTO SAFETY.

We hear it in life all the time "if you want to be successful in life you need to be fearless, if you're not going to be fearless you're not going to win." When you break down and understand the definition of each word you'll understand what I'm about to break down and tell you that "fearless" is inaccurate. It's misleading and it doesn't make a lot of sense. See, fearless is having no fear, a lack of fear and in life that's not reality.

In life, we're going to have fear. In fact we're going to have fear barriers come at us all the time. Especially if we're the type of person, and most of us are, that are growing, expanding and staying on that cutting edge of life all the time. When you live in that space the fear barriers are going to come at you like waves. Also understand if you're that type of person that just likes to sit back idle on the sidelines and kind of watch life go by and stay in your safety zone as much as you can - you're still going to be hit with fear barriers. No matter what, fear is part of life it's just part of the journey. Understanding the definitions will really help you create an overall understanding of why I believe "fearless" is misleading and is just not correct.

The word "courage" is based on the Latin word "cor" and that means coming from the inside, coming from the heart, coming from the soul. When you can do that and identify that, well that courageousness is really what you want to go for. That's real, that's what's going to get you through those fear barriers. Being courageous does not mean having a lack of fear in fact it's really the flip-side. Being courageous really means you are afraid but you're still moving forward, you're not letting it stop you. That's really courageous. That's the ultimate goal and the state you really want to be in on a consistent basis in your life because when you can do that your life becomes limitless. The possibilities for your life become endless because you're not going to let those fear barriers stop you. Again I want to be crystal clear on those definitions and not have you be confused on being fearless because "fearless" just does not exist in our lives.

I like to use high-end athletes as an example a lot of the time when it comes to personal development. The number one reason is because when you get to know them behind the scenes, behind that black curtain, you're going to understand every high-end athlete uses personal development on a consistent basis whether they realize it or not. That's the only way you're going to get to that high-end level in a sport, you have to use certain things and take certain steps. Again, sometimes they might not be able to define it as personal development but it absolutely is personal development.

High-end athletes come across fear barriers all the time and they have to learn how to manage those and how to break through those fear barriers. They have to really learn how to be courageous to break through those fears and get to that next level. They keep pushing themselves in order to stay on top because when you're on top, other people are constantly trying to get there. That's why there's a difference between a champion and a contender. The champion has learned how to break through those fear barriers and how to stay in that courageous state. They learned how to understand and embrace fear; it's started to become a part of their journey.

Another great example of courageous are soldiers out in a war zone. I remember I was married at the time and my father-in-law was a Viet Nam vet and he was First Force Recon in Viet Nam. He was a Marine. I used to listen to his stories; I loved when he would share his stories. I'd just sit there and listen and be in awe of this man the things he'd accomplished, the things he did and the things he just had to get through in his life especially in Viet Nam. I remember, I was probably 24 or 25 years old and we were just sitting and talking one day and he started telling stories and I said "You know Jim, I always wonder what I would do as a man, how I would handle those situations." I was never at war I was never in the military so I wondered if I would have been able to handle that situation, what would I do in some of those situations. He didn't blink an eye he just said "You'd be fine." I asked him how he knew that and he said "first of all I know who you are and I know your character. Secondly, you don't do it for you; you do it for him and him and him."

I had never thought about it that way because I'd never been in that situation but it makes a lot of sense. You're talking about life and death decisions, life and death situations. You're scared to death; you are completely and utterly scared to death wondering if you're going to make it the next minute the next second, the next day, the next month. Are you going to lose a limb? Are you going to lose your life? Is the guy or girl next to you going to lose their life or lose a limb? You're constantly in that fearful state. But because something is bigger than you, you create that courageous state to get you through that moment and get you through that time.

When they're walking through the jungle and they're not sure what's going to be around the corner, if they take a left or a right what's going to be around the bend. Take it a step further and with First Force Recon there are usually four and not more than six men that are dropped off within an area that we've never been in. So they've got to navigate and radio back for the rest of the team. When he told me that's how they get through those times it all came back to you can't go into a war unless you're courageous. No one in their right mind would go into a war in a fearless state, it's impossible because you don't know what's going to happen. This is life and death. You tap into that courageous state it's not about me it's about that guy next to me; my brother to the left of me and my brother to the right of me or my sister to the left of me and my sister to the right of me. That's why they call it a brotherhood. There are situations you're only going to be able to get through by tapping into that courageous state.

It also relates to business owners, entrepreneurs because it's such a lonely, lonely title. Being an entrepreneur today has a lot of hype behind it, a lot of bells and whistles. Young people are starting these companies and getting a lot of money and thinking it's so cool to be an entrepreneur right now. But at the end of the day being a real, true entrepreneur is a lonely life for a big percentage of your life because you're always going after goals that scare and excite you at the same time and most people aren't going to be able to relate to those goals. Even in your inner circle they're going to think you're a little crazy, they're going to wonder why you're doing this. To not only survive but to thrive as an entrepreneur you're going to have to learn to tap into that courageous state. If you don't, you're going to back into safety and stop growing. Remember we're either growing and moving forward or staying safe and moving backwards. We never stay exactly the same.

As an entrepreneur a few things happen, you feel like you're by yourself a lot of times you feel like you're on an island. Only you understand and only you get it, right? There are also times where things are going well but in order to keep them going well you have to stay on the cutting edge of your industry. In order to do that you have to be willing to step outside your comfort zone get back into that darkness until it gets familiar and you become comfortable then you do it all over again. It's a repetitive cycle in order to stay on top, in order to keep growing and in order to keep moving forward you have to learn to get into that courageous state and not stay in that fearful state. There might be times you do stay in that fearful state and it moves you back into safety but as long as you don't stay there and you get back out and get back up and dust yourself off and keep moving forward things start to unfold. I always say that action is fear's kryptonite. When you take consistent action things start to happen. We're going to get into that in another chapter much, much deeper in action, what it takes and what it's all about.

But in this chapter, fearless vs. courageous is so vitally important to really understand because when you can raise your level of awareness, when you know you're in that fearful state you have the wherewithal to get into that courageous state and break through. That's really what it boils down to. The people who don't work on themselves, who don't have personal development skills in their toolbox, most likely they're going to go back into safety. If you go back to those soldiers, boot camp, all the training they've done conditions them to get into that courageous state. Again, whether they can define it or not that's really what it is. All their training makes it second nature. You know, "react this way because this is what our training was all about."

Really, when you break it down to its simplest form it's all about how to get out of that fearful state and get into that courageous state so you can break through those fear barriers. So you can keep moving forward. When you're talking about life and death situations - listen the person next to you could die, you could die if you don't get into that courageous state. There are times when you can't run and if you do run it's only going to be for so long when you're talking about life and death situations. Even in athletics, you can only run away for so long until you're going to have to step up or get out. As an entrepreneur you're going to have to figure out how to tap into that courageous state and keep moving forward even when you don't have the money. When you just don't have the finances and the bills are piling up and there's not enough business coming in. When your family is on you to get out, to abandon what you're doing because to them it just doesn't look healthy, it doesn't look right, they don't like how things are going. That's when all the fear comes in and really starts to suppress you unless you can get into that courageous state. The courageous state is the only way to get out of that fearful state. And understanding that "fearless" is really nonsense it holds no water in the real world.

Fearless vs. courageous also taps into your life, your personal life. If you are a parent raising your kids and you're so fearful something bad's going to happen, you need to understand your job as a parent is to raise the most competent adults that you can. So you have to let them try things and stay in that courageous state so you can let them fall down. Listen, if they fall down and they get back up it's going to build their character and who they are which in turn makes you become a better parent because you're really doing your job. Your job is to create a competent, self-assured, self-reliant, young adult. That's really your job in those first 18 years, to mold a capable individual who's going to give back to society instead of just taking from society. But because you love your child so much you want to protect them, that's second nature. You have to learn how to let go of that fearful state get into that courageous state and know you're doing the right thing for your child because that is your job.

If you want to lose weight, get into shape and you've never done it before you're going to have so much fear and anxiety going into that gym. Same with figuring out how to eat right or work out right or what things you should implement and how to implement them or how to create a daily routine and new lifestyle. I promise you, I used to be a personal trainer, you can't stay in that fearful state; you have to learn how to get into that courageous state. A great way to get into that courageous state, and stay there, is to surround yourself with the right people. When I was a personal trainer I would constantly pull people through their fear barriers, like not knowing if they could do it or just not knowing how they were going to do it. I would pull them through their fear barriers by showing them what to do and being there for them and supporting them. So again, whether it's personal, professional, physical or something else doesn't matter we're going to have fear barriers every single day. They're going to come at us like waves. We need to learn how to recognize when we're in that fearful state and how to identify it because if you can't identify it you can't fix it.

So identify when you're in that fearful state, identify that it's normal, it's natural to have that fearful state. Then what do we do to conquer that? You have to figure out whatever that circumstance is for you at that time then figure out how to get into that courageous state in order to break through that fear barrier. Surrounding yourself with the right people especially in the beginning is vital. A lot of times when it's so brand new to you surrounding yourself with the right people is going to be a make or break decision. There are times when if you don't have those people who have been there backing you, supporting you, there is a chance you're going to go back into safety because that's our natural thought process. Unless you change that thought paradigm you're going to go back into safety where it feels better.

The problem with safety is it only feels better for a short period of time. Then it becomes so toxic, so counter-productive because you stop growing, you stop learning. We're here on earth to grow, to learn, evolve and move forward. That's the bottom line. When we don't do that is when other things start to set in - your subconscious reminds you that you couldn't crash through that fear barrier. So, as a human you start looking

for other outlets to feel better and a lot of times those other outlets are really toxic like drinking, drugs or gambling just for the feeling of release or escaping.

You know over the years I've changed my paradigm. Over the past 17 years my outlet has been the gym which has actually been a healthy outlet. A lot of people don't have that level of awareness because they haven't put the time into their personal development. Understand that when you go back into safety it's only a short-term fix, right, it's only a band aid on a real wound. You have to learn how to sew that wound up so it doesn't keep bleeding and it starts to heal. It you just keep putting a band aid on it and it's a bad enough wound it's not going to heal or if it does it's not going to heal correctly. That goes back into your subconscious mind because your subconscious mind reminds you that you didn't do it.

That then creates a dent, a kink in your armor, when it comes to yourself image because you keep reminding yourself that you couldn't do it. That leads to thinking you can't be good enough that you might not be smart enough. You start telling yourself you might not been good looking enough or you're too fat or too skinny or you don't have enough experience and on and on. Understand where it starts from, it starts from not being able to break through those fear barriers going back into safety. It's a trickle-down effect that ultimately stops at your foundation, your self-image. We're going to dive into self-image in chapter 8 really, really deep. Self-image is everything.

Fearless is inaccurate, don't even worry about being fearless. It's all about being courageous. When you're courageous and you get into that courageous state you will win long term. That's what high-end athletes do, that's what soldiers do, and that's what successful entrepreneurs do. That's also what successful parents do, what people in successful relationships do. It doesn't really matter what area of your life, when you look back now that you understand this a little bit better and you start to dissect either yourself or other people you're going to find the same recipe just different ingredients. So "fearless" means nothing, courageous is the state you want to live your life in because it comes from the inside and that's long-lasting.

ROUND 4

THIS AIN'T BATMAN & ROBIN.

IF IT DON'T SCARE AND EXCITE YOU AT THE SAME TIME, IT JUST AIN'T BIG ENOUGH.

Goals. Goals that scare you and excite you at the same time. You know I always talk about this, there's a difference between setting goals and achieving goals. One of my mentors, Bob Proctor, told me a long time ago, "you know, Dave, setting goals is an intellectual process but achieving goals is a lawful process." What he meant by that is that setting a goal, an idea, is sort of coming from the outside - it's an intellectual process it's a thought it's an idea. But achieving goals is a whole other animal if you will. What he meant by "lawful process" is that there are laws in the universe that dictate what we do and what we don't do, what we can do and what we can't do. Now once you learn and understand these laws you can utilize them, leverage them, and create them to be your best friend rather than your worst enemy. To give an example let's take the Law of Gravity. If you climb up a ladder and jump off you're going to fall because the Law of Gravity says so. That is just one of the laws in the universe that dictate how we live. We can learn how to work with these laws rather than against them.

The process of setting goals is pretty simple, it's really very easy and people do it all the time. But, do they really achieve them? When they fall short, why is that? That's what I'm going to talk to you about in this chapter. Again, starting off before anything else, you have to ask yourself "does my goal, does my end destination, have that dynamic duo? Does it scare me and excite me at the same time?" If it doesn't, you need to stop and go back and find something that does because it's not going to keep your attention or give you enough juice to get you up out of bed in the morning. If it doesn't, you won't keep that focus or keep that drive.

Understand something it needs to ultimately give you that need or fulfillment or happiness. Everyone says, "Just be happy. Everything's OK if you're just happy." Well there's a little bit more to it than that. Happiness is based entirely on and completely tied in with fulfillment.   If we feel fulfilled in whatever it is the byproduct is being happy. Not the other way around.   So whether that is personal, physical, spiritual, professional, or all of the above, whatever pillar that is in your life understand it starts with figuring out what is really going to mean something to you. What is really going to be fulfilling to you? Because the happiness, the monetary stuff, the success will all follow that fulfillment. So that dynamic duo of being scared and excited at the same time is a must and really is the starting point of everything that goes with setting and achieving goals.

Now, there is something called "Smart Goals" and for each letter of the word "smart" there's a title and for each title there's a definition and a little more explanation. So, I'm going to break these down and get into each one of these letters and why it's important to set smart goals. Obviously the word "smart" begins with "S" so let's start there.   S means specific, your goals must be specific. Clarity is power. You have to be specific in setting your goals. You need to have that clear roadmap. Now this doesn't mean you know exactly how you're going to get there, but you need a starting point. You also need a mid-point and an end-point. So you'll need to set short, medium and long-term goals.   I'll get into that a little deeper as well later in this chapter. Remember being specific is key in your starting point. You have to be clear, it doesn't mean as you keep moving forward you're not going to tweak things or change things here and there as you are going but being specific to that end goal is vitally important to not only get started but to stay on track and to ultimately reach your goal.

The "M" in smart goals is meaningful. We've already talked a little about this it has to mean something to you. Your goal has to create an emotion, a feeling that you get when you think about, when you talk about and when you start moving toward this goal, this destination. It has to have that "juice" it has to keep your focus and I believe this is a big reason why or at least one of the reasons why so many people set out at the beginning of the year making resolutions they don't keep. They start out all excited but deep down their resolutions don't really mean enough to them, there's not enough feeling or emotion to carry them through. Plus they probably didn't set those short, medium and long-term goals and probably weren't specific enough. When you're not specific enough you're not going to keep that focus, that drive. Getting back to "meaning" though, your goal has to wake you up, keep you focused, keep you excited and keep you passionate about what you're doing or it's not big enough. It's not going to be worth it to you when you hit those struggles and obstacles to keep going toward your goal.

The "A" in smart goals is for "action." Action oriented. You can have the greatest ideas but nothing happens until you start to take that action. Action means everything. Action also means that you're going to make mistakes and fall down, but you're going to learn from it and just don't keep making the same mistakes. Again this is where so many people fall down they don't realize action is everything. Either they don't take any action and just keep talking about it and analyzing it - you know the analysis of paralysis. Or they take lots of action but there's no direction no meaning and all of a sudden it goes away. That's what happens so often with the New Year's resolutions. People get all excited for the first few days, maybe just the first few hours maybe the first few weeks. Then all of a sudden, those resolutions just disappear because they're not setting their goals and achieving their goals in that lawful process, in a real specific way. So action is everything. Everything happens around action in your life, every single one of those pillars - spiritual, personal, professional, physical, whatever it is it doesn't matter action dictates everything.

The "R" in smart goals is for "rewarding." Again, this is meaningful, fulfillment, passion-related, it all ties in with obtaining those goals that are big enough. For a lot of people this goes along with helping others. Is your goal going to help others? A lot of the time that's what people are looking for. Understand they better you make yourself the better people around you are going to be. So, it's not about being selfish, it's about starting with you first so that everyone around you can be a better version of themselves because you are a better version of yourself. Rewarding, uplifting, meaningful, fulfillment, all different titles but they all go back to and are anchored by the same foundation. That foundation is the feelings, the emotions, the "how does it make me feel." If it doesn't make you feel good, stop doing it.

That's not saying when you're taking on those short-term goals you're going to love every second of it. It's not about that. But if it doesn't fulfill you on a consistent basis it probably means you should consider doing something else. If it does and you are consistently taking those action steps and you're not loving every single part of it understand that's just the way it is. That's life.

The "T" in smart goals stands for "time-sensitive." We talked about being specific but you also need to put start date and an end date to every one of your goals. This is vitally important because it gives you direction and a sense of accomplishment when you hit that end date. The start date? You're not going to be able to take any action if you don't know when you're starting out. A lot of times it's also a good idea to put a mid-date down. So now you can evaluate, you can audit how you're doing. You can look back and see how far you've come and how much farther you have to go to get to that finish date.

So, let's start with the short-term goals. On a daily basis I put together what I call a "victory list." A victory list is really a to do list, but I call it a victory list because every time I accomplish one of the things on that list I put a big "v" next to it because subconsciously it empowers me. I feel a real sense of accomplishment rather than just crossing it off the list and moving down. Try it and see how that works for you. It really works for me and it was taught to me by Jack Canfield years ago and I've never stopped using it.

Each night I write down my victory list for the following day but before I do that I evaluate what on that day's list I've accomplished and those things I haven't accomplished I just move to the next day. I write my victory list down, however many things are on the list, in order of importance. I prioritize them so that number 1 is a high priority and number 10 is probably a lower priority. At the end of the day when I evaluate, a lot of time I look back at my day and I call this the entrepreneurial DNA, we always feel like we need to do more, like we haven't done enough. That's just part of who we are, that's what gets us to obtain our goals a lot of the time, that self-drive. But sometimes I look back at my day and I see I didn't do everything I wanted to do and I don't feel like I did enough. So I look back at my victory list and I might have started the day out with 12 things on that list and maybe I got 10 of them done. Then I realize I had more of a productive day than I thought. Again, this will give you a sense of accomplishment. Or, I could look back and say "gee, why did I only get four of these things done?" Maybe it was because two of them took much longer than I thought or maybe I lost my focus. Maybe I lost my drive for a period of time during that day. The great thing about it though is once you've identified it you can fix it and move forward. It's not about beating yourself up; it's about auditing yourself so you know exactly where you are throughout the whole process.

Let's talk about mid-term goals and why I think they're so important. Mid-term goals give you a point where you look around and look back to see how much you've accomplished and how much you've grown as a person to get to that point and now what do you need to do in order to move forward to get to your end destination. These mid-term goals are often overlooked, they're not utilized and I think it's just a huge, powerful tool when you're working toward a goal that has that dynamic duo.

Lastly is your end goal that end destination, your deadline if you will. Having an end goal is vitally important so you know when you get there. This is like calling yourself out, drawing a line in the sand you're saying "this will be accomplished on this date." Understand, if you don't get it all accomplished by that date give yourself a break, take a step back and audit everything it took to get you to that point to that level. Even though you didn't accomplish everything you wanted just sit back and reevaluate and learn from your experience before you move on. Then set another end date and keep moving forward until you get there. It pulls you through the whole time and gives you direction and a sense of accomplishment. It gives you a reason "why." It's all tied in when you set short, medium and long-term goals.

Feeling fulfilled is a huge part of your life in obtaining happiness, whatever that means to you on any of those pillars: personal, professional, physical, spiritual it's all the same thing. By setting those goals you're going to live a much more fulfilled life. We are put on this earth for one thing and one thing only - to grow, evolve and move forward. When you can do that you're going to live an amazing life. How many people do you know that worked their whole life either for themselves or for an organization and because they were so involved in what they did for all of those years it sort of became part of their identity?

Then when they retired or sold that business it looked like all the air was just taken out of them? Why? Because we need that purpose in our life, we need that juice; we need that goal that destination to feel like we're living. That is why when parents let their whole world revolve around their kids and the kids move out they feel depleted. It's because they put all their energy and focus on their kids and forgot about themselves. After the kids leave the parents have to reinvent themselves, figure out what their purpose is in this life. It doesn't matter how old or young you are, we all need that in our lives to actually live what I consider a good quality of life. There are a lot of people just going through the motions. That's really not quality. They just keep doing it year after year and they call it living. To me that's being robotic, you're really dying; you're just taking a long time to actually get there.

I want to share this story with you; in 2005 I was very fortunate to have met a gentleman named Jack Lalanne. Now if you're not familiar with Jack Lalanne you should google him, he's an amazing man. He was the first person to have a fitness TV show back in the late 40's and early 50's when television first came out. Then he opened up gyms across the country, he franchised his gyms and he was just an amazing businessman; but even more than that he was just an amazing person who changed and enhanced so many lives. When I met him in 2005 he was 92 years old. One of the things he's known for is when he was 70 or 72 years old he swam the Pacific Ocean by San Francisco pulling a boat. I forget how long of a swim this was but it was absolutely unbelievable, against the current, at 70 or 72 years old. At 92 years old when I met him I was in Columbus, Ohio at a professional body building show and he was getting a lifetime achievement award from Arnold Schwarzenegger. When I met Jack Lalanne, he was 92 years old but he had more energy, his mind was so clear to converse with him was absolutely amazing. He got on stage and Arnold was about to introduce him and couldn't find him. He had so much energy he was just running around the place, flexing and having a great time with the crowd. Arnold couldn't even keep up with the guy. Now that's what I talking about with quality of life! Jack Lalanne never lost his purpose or his sense of fulfillment. That's part of goal setting, that's part of living a really full life.

Make sure you write down your goals. Follow the S.M.A.R.T. formula. When you do this, and you set those short, medium and long-term goals you will eventually get where you want to go. If you stay on course and let this process work for you and with you, you will absolutely get there. To become the person you need to grow to be to hit that end goal, there's just no other way to do it than to set short, medium and long-term goals and keep moving forward. You can't get that strength of character, that strength of self-image in a classroom. You can't even get it in a book. You can learn things of course, but life, real applied steps that's what's going to get you there. That's what is going to create that wisdom that only people who have been there and done that can acquire. There's not a classroom or book in this world that's going to give you the wisdom life gives you. Plus you're not going to get there without learning the difference between setting and achieving goals, the lawful process and the steps it's going to take to get you there.

ROUND 5

THE HOW DON'T MATTER.

DON'T WORRY ABOUT HOW AS LONG
AS THE WHY IS BIG ENOUGH.

What we're going to talk about in this chapter is really the foundation of everything, no matter what you want to do in life this is the foundation. We're going to really dive into "why" because your "why" is the very foundation of everything you do. Identifying your "why" how important it is to identify your "why" and the power than comes when you do identify your "why" correctly all make up that foundation.

When you have a goal that scares and excites you at the same time you have a why that's big enough to pull you through those fear barriers. If you don't have a why that's big enough to pull you through those fear barriers those fear barriers will stop you every time and pull you back into safety and you're going to stop growing. When your why becomes big enough it becomes the power that's going to pull you through. If you want to take it a step further, when your why becomes bigger than you are you become unstoppable. Let me repeat that, when your why becomes bigger than you, you become unstoppable.

You know, I talk about this in my keynote but when I left construction and was looking for work and answered an ad in the paper for an outside sales job when I was 20 or 21 years old I couldn't identify it then. But I can certainly identify it now. There were certain steps I took without even realizing it to get me through those fear barriers, the unknown, being outside of my comfort zone. One of the biggest steps that I took that I created without even realizing it at the time was creating a "why" that was big enough.

Now I was 20, 21, years old and I was renting a room from my buddy's mom and I was looking for work. I'd been in construction at the time and we were going through a major, major recession economically and I was going from jobsite to jobsite and there was just nothing going on for construction labor. Jobsites were being shut down, money was tight, banks weren't lending. At that time it was way before the internet so for those of you out there who don't remember, we had to get a paper and look for a job in the help wanted ads. So there I am on a Monday morning in the kitchen looking through the help wanted ads for something in construction. Page 1, nothing. Page 2, nothing. Page 3, not a single job that fits my criteria. So I go back to page 1 thinking maybe I missed something. I'm half way through page 1 and all of a sudden I see this ad - it just jumps right out at me. It says "Outside sales, selling copiers and fax machines b to b." At that time I knew absolutely nothing about outside sales and while I knew what copiers and fax machines were I didn't know enough to sell them, and "b to b?" I didn't even know what that meant at the time. But right underneath in big bold letters it said "no experience necessary, will train." I thought I was a great candidate for that because, well, that was my resume at the time.

I had no experience and needed someone to train me in something so I answer that ad. I picked up the phone and dialed that number. I was in the kitchen by myself and that big green fear barrier monster was staring me down. It took everything I could muster to make the appointment, go to the interview and actually talk to the boss about a job. Remember I was a laborer. I didn't think I belonged there. I was looking at that door the whole time I was filling out the application, I was ready to make a run for it. Even during the interview my old conditioning came rushing right back in bring that fear barrier right back with it. I didn't want to move, I didn't want to touch anything. All I could do was look around that big office.

When Tommy came into the interview and started asking questions that fear barrier just intensified. Then it intensified again when Tommy took me to buy my suits. Really Tommy's sort of demented sense of humor - he liked to see people squirm - really added even more fear to the mix. I was way out of my comfort zone for sure. Driving home from that event that fear barrier was really bearing down on me. I was in complete darkness. I was nowhere near my comfort zone! My first day on the job was the next morning. I had no idea what I was in for, when Tommy asked me about cold calling I didn't have a clue what he was talking about. I just made the decision to follow Tommy around like a little puppy and try to soak up as much knowledge as I could.

Back in the first chapter I told the story of the attorney firm in the big office building in Center City, Philly when Tommy left me on my own to get the decision maker's name. I was really intimidated by the whole scene, the receptionists, the entry way to the office, the wrap around aquarium. Even after I got the decision maker's card I still wanted to just run. It took a lot for me to just walk out of that office, even at a brisk walk. But I'd done it. Tommy knew I could do it and I did it. That was a real confidence builder for me, I could do this. Tommy knew exactly what he was doing and of course he did get his money back for those suits.

I share this story again because of how beautifully it shows how important identifying your why really is. If you look back at this story, all the fear I experienced during different parts of this story, how was I even able to stay in that lobby filling out the paperwork when I really wanted to run out the door. Why didn't I just run out of there? How was I even able to make the initial phone call to make the appointment for the interview when I was scared to death? I didn't even want to say hello. How was I able to make the phone call and be able to speak? Why didn't I run out of that attorney's firm when I realized Tommy wasn't there? Because my why was big enough. I was able to make that phone call and I was able to stay in that lobby because my why was big enough. I had no job, no money and bills right around the corner. I had to eat, pay bills and survive. So my why was plenty big enough at that time to pull me through those fear barriers when I had no idea where I was, where I was going and was completely in the dark. My why pulled me through.

If you want to take it a step further, how was I able to cold-call that attorney's firm when Tommy left me and we'd only worked together for a week and a half before that? Because my why at that moment actually became bigger than me. My why was about never ever letting Tommy down. I would have walked through fire for Tommy at that time. What you have to understand is up to that point in my life Tommy was the first successful adult that told me they believed in me and showed me they believed in me. That man bought me three shirts, three suits and three ties and he'd known me for about three hours.

All the outside noise and everything I brought to the table, which wasn't much, looking at me on paper I had no business being there. I had no outside sales experience, no experience at all in his industry, never graduated high school, and I'd only been a construction laborer up to that point. Really I had no business being there at all but Tommy saw something in me and he took a chance. So there was no way I would let Tommy down. I would have walked through fire for that man at that time. That's how powerful, that's how important identifying your why is.

So when you hit those road blocks, when you hit those rough times, when you feel like there's nothing left you feel like you're completely depleted, there's no way out, there are no answers, remember we've all been there. If you're willing to grow and expand and move forward it's going to hit you much more than someone who is going to just stand on the sidelines and watch the game being played and not get in. That's not what this book is about. This book is for people who want to get in the game, are not afraid to get dirty, not afraid to get knocked down. Those people who get back up, brush themselves off and keep moving forward - that's who this book is for. That's what this book is about. That's what I identify with because that's been my life. So, that being said when your why becomes bigger than you, you literally become unstoppable.

All because my why was big enough I never went back into construction. Tommy made me believe that I could do it. There were certain things I couldn't identify then that we're now talking about in this book. It's always the same recipe, just different ingredients no matter what it is that you're doing whether it's personal, professional, physical or spiritual. I don't care what pillar it is or if it's all of them it's always the same recipe just different ingredients. That's why it's so important to completely understand this chapter. When you hit those road blocks, those fear barriers, your why is going to pull you through.

Picture yourself in the ocean. You're way out in the ocean the waves are coming at you and pushing you under. You're fighting to get air. They're pushing you under and you're fighting to get air. Your why becomes your safety. It's like the Coast Guard throwing out the dingy, coming to your rescue. We've all been there, especially entrepreneurs who find themselves in debt and by themselves, those single moms trying to feed her three kids and hold down a job, or that kid trying to get through school who just doesn't get it and can't learn in that certain way. It can feel like you're in the middle of the ocean and the waves just keep pushing you under. When you can identify your why it becomes your safety net. Your why becomes that safety boat you can jump in or hold on to until you can start to paddle through those waves.

I wanted to give you a vision of this because we think in pictures. As I tell you about the middle of the ocean, you see yourself in the middle of the ocean. When I'm explaining the waves coming at you like fear barriers, you can see yourself being pushed under and fighting to get air. That fighting to get air is survival. So your why is going to be that dingy, that safety boat. That is how vitally important your why is.

I think the reason a lot of people who have enough courage to set goals that scare and excite them at the same time but can't identify their why is because it's not concrete enough for them. By the way, your why doesn't have to mean anything to anyone else and most of the time it won't. It only has to mean something to you. It has to be deeply rooted in your soul to get you through. Again I would have walked through fire for that man at that time because of the belief he instilled in me and felt for me.

We are all passionate, energy-based human beings. That's how we're built. We all are. Some people show it differently than others. I am very, very passionate and I'm a very emotionally articulate speaker. I talk with my hands a lot. There are other people who are also very, very passionate about things and have a very deep-seated why but they just present it differently. They are more reserved. This doesn't mean things don't feel any different for you than it does for them or for me. It's just your personality.

That's very important to understand. Passion doesn't always mean an out-going person. Passion is what something means to you inside, what does it mean inside your heart and soul. That's where your why is imbedded that's where inspiration comes from - your why. I wanted to share this because it's just so important to figure out what your why is. When you can identify your why it creates a road map, it gives you direction along with setting a goal that scares and excites you at the same time. Those two things together, your why and a big enough goal, really do give you a roadmap you can start to navigate with the proper action. So lean on your why, always, always lean on that why. It's so important. If your why isn't big enough, it just doesn't give you enough juice. If it doesn't give you goosebumps you need to stop immediately and go find that why that does give you that feeling. It doesn't matter what your why is, you could want to lose weight, get in shape, change your whole lifestyle. There are people out there who have never lived a healthy lifestyle, all of a sudden they're in their mid 40's or 50's and they have a heart condition or diabetes or some other health condition. That could be their why. They don't want to die. That why is big enough to get them to sign up for the gym, start to eat healthy, and start to educate themselves. Then there are those other people in the same circumstance and that same why isn't big enough for them to make changes and they end up dying or living with chronic health issues. It all depends on you. What is your why?

When I was introduced to personal development 17 or 18 years ago when I first started to learn we're all energy and about the mindset my biggest why was that I wanted to change my life. I did not like the direction my life was going in and had been going in for a while. I saw this as my savior, personal development made so much sense to me I became completely infatuated and I still am today. I always want to keep learning about personal development, about the mindset, about paradigm shifts and energy, about the thoughts we think and why we think them. All of this combined. I just can't get enough of personal development because of the changes it's made in my life. So that why will be with me until the day I die.

That why is so big for me it just can't get any bigger. It's my life, it's my oxygen.

One example for me is working out. I love working out. My alarm goes off at 4:30 every morning and I'm at the gym unless I'm bedridden, sick or traveling. I'm at that gym because that's my iron therapy. That's my zen. People ask me how I keep going to the gym and how I do it every day and it's because it's my lifestyle and that ties in to my why. My why is so big because of the feeling I get, the clarity I get when I'm in the gym. When I leave the gym I'm a different person from the one I was when I walked in. I've been an athlete my whole life and I love it.

I had a really bad motorcycle accident about 17 or 18 years ago where I almost died or could have been paralyzed. I was in intensive care for four or five days because I'd broken everything on my right side and had punctured a lung. I could have broken my neck if I'd hit differently. That made me realize tomorrow isn't guaranteed for any of us. I almost had my why, working out, taken away from me. From that point on I never missed a workout unless I'm traveling and I'll still figure out a way to work out. Or if I'm bedridden or sick with the flu or something like that. Other than those instances I've never missed a workout.

Now anytime I'm stressed or setting new goals or have a business I'm working on, a lot of balls in the air, I actually start implementing two workouts a day. I'll go in the afternoon too and break up my day. I'll get up at 4:30 in the morning and get my breakfast ready, my pre-workout mean, get my pre-workout drink and get in the gym, get that sweat and clear my head. That gets me ready for my day. Then anywhere from 4:30 to 6:30 in the afternoon I'll go right back to the gym and get another workout in, clear my head again. Then I go back to my home office, get a shower, eat dinner and then I'm ready for another four or five hours of work if I need to. By doing this I chop up my day and it completely changes my mindset. It really clears all the nonsense out it's like doing spring cleaning twice a day between my ears. Again, that's my why. I get so much more done and I just feel better overall. I feel stronger, I feel more vibrant and I turn the clock back. I'll be 50 years old this September, 2016 and I feel like I'm in my 20's. That's always been my goal. I never wanted to feel my age and I certainly don't want to feel older. I always want to feel 10, 15 maybe even 20 years younger than I am.

To me there's a difference between quality and quantity. For me it's all about quality of life. I don't know how long I'm going to be here. You don't know how long you're going to be here. So start identifying your why, set goals that give you some juice, and lean on that why. Identify your why and I'm telling you if it's not big enough go find something that is. I hope this chapter really sent it home on how important that why is and how to identify that why. It is absolutely the foundation to build on with anything you want in your life.

Now this doesn't mean your why can't be tweaked. It doesn't even mean your why isn't going to be tweaked. As a matter of fact, if your goal is big enough and it's going to take you a long enough time to get there your why is going to be tweaked or added to and that's ok. Understand successful people have to be able to adapt to things that come at them in life. The most successful people, if you really analyze them, can adapt on a dime. They can change direction on a dime because they've built that ability. They've used that muscle over and over. That's the way you not only survive but you thrive not only in business but in life in general. Make sure you identify that why, make sure it's big enough and if it can become bigger than you, you will be unstoppable if you keep seeing it through and you lean on that why. I hope this helps and I'll see you in the next chapter!

ROUND 6

PACK IT
IN IF YOU
WON'T
DO THIS.

ACTION BECOMES MAGICAL — AS YOU TAKE THE ACTION,
THE PEOPLE AND CIRCUMSTANCES APPEAR
TO MAKE IT HAPPEN.

This chapter is vitally, vitally important not only to understand but to apply. In this chapter we're going to talk about action. You know, you can do everything right. You can have the best business plan, the best people around you, you can have all your ducks in a row, you can cross all your "t's" and dot all your "i's" and be ready and be ready and be ready but never take action. If you're not going to take action nothing happens. If you're not going to take action just pack it in because it's not going to work. Action, perspiration, is a must in anything that you do. Especially if you're in the business world, if you're an entrepreneur or you're a leader or manager. Whatever you do to make a living you have to take action.

So many people, when they create something new, come up against a big fear barrier. There are those "what ifs" or "suppose I fail" or the fear of success or any number of other fear barriers. Those fear barriers start to creep in and they stop taking action or they take no action at all. They keep planning and planning and planning. It's kind of like in the real estate world they call it the analysis of paralysis, you keep looking over the numbers and looking over the numbers and looking over the data, the paperwork. All you're doing is subconsciously buying more time so you don't have to take that action. So you don't have to go into that scary darkness. You have to understand though, when you enter into that darkness it's only temporary as long as you keep moving forward and taking action. The whole key to undoing those fears is action, action, action. Action is the kryptonite to fear. Even if you take the wrong action, just get back up and maybe you have to go back and move left instead of right or right instead of left but keep getting back up. You have to learn how to evaluate so you're not constantly taking wrong action, but if you keep moving forward the right people and circumstances start to come into your life.

Life becomes magical when you take action. The whole universe, the sun, the moon and the stars start to align when you take action. The whole universe starts to help you get to where you need to go. Make no mistake though it's a double-edged sword, if you stop taking action the right people and circumstances stop appearing. I share a story in my keynote, and I've shared it in this book too - the Tommy story. The bottom line here is that I needed work, no job, no money, bills right around the corner. I had to eat, pay bills and survive. So when I was calling for that outside sales job that I saw in the paper I was scared to death but I kept taking that action because my why was big enough. As I kept taking action, as I kept moving forward the people and the circumstances started to come into my life to make it unfold, to make it happen.

See Tommy was my very first mentor in business ever. When I answered that ad and started to work for him I couldn't identify it then. But I can identify it now. The only reason I met Tommy, the only reason I had that opportunity to get out of the construction industry, move up, grow and expand is solely because I took that action. Understand I also had a big enough why because I had to eat, pay bills and survive - yes my why was plenty big enough. I could lean on that why while I was taking that action and going through that darkness, that fear barrier, that scary, scary time being out of my comfort zone.

Another story I share is when I first moved from New Jersey to San Diego I didn't know what business I was going to do. So I found a struggling sports nutrition store. When I evaluated what they were doing and why they were struggling I saw some things in the marketing and the branding end of things that I thought I could implement that they weren't doing and I thought those things would pay off. Understand I'd just relocated to San Diego from New Jersey in July of 2008. By November of 2008 I had signed the deal and purchased the store. I knew nobody in San Diego or even in California. This was a brand new industry for me. I did know a little bit about the supplement side of the sports nutrition industry but I'd never had a brick and mortar retail business before. Plus if you remember 2007, 2008 and 2009 there was a recession going on. Now I know they called it a recession but for a lot of people it was a complete depression.

Everyone around me in my inner circle thought I was crazy, they thought I'd completely lost my mind. They were reminding me I'd just relocated across the country, didn't really know anyone in the area, never had a sports nutrition business and the country was in the worst financial crisis in probably 30 years. I just kept taking the action because my why was big enough. I kept leaning on my why. It had to work, I had such a passion for the industry, and I saw things the previous owner wasn't doing that I thought I could implement. With a lot of blood, sweat and tears within the first year and a half I literally tripled the numbers in that economy, not knowing anybody in the area and with a business that was new to me.

What had happened was I'd put together a basic game plan, in my head and not even on paper and I just started taking action. I started wading into the water if you will. You know when you're walking up to the ocean and you start feeling that cold water. You're up to your ankles then up to your knees. You're shivering and shaking. Walk back out, step back out, and then run as fast as you can into that ocean! It's going to be much, much better than just tiptoeing in. I'm big about the thinking you should jump off the cliff and build the plane on the way down. In my opinion that's when you know you really have the entrepreneurial DNA. If you really can't do that, you might want to rethink being a full-time entrepreneur because so many things are going to come up.

When you're taking action you have to be able to change on a dime. You have to be able to change your plan if it's not working. You have to be able to step back and say "ok, let me try this..." But it's a dance, you also have to give it enough time. I'll give you an example. I'd tripled the business of my sports nutrition store within a year and a half. My original plan was to have three or four stores all around southern California but I saw most of the business in that industry was heading away from brick and mortar stores and towards online sales. But the franchise prohibited individual stores from selling online. In order for me to get to that point I had to take a lot of action. Then I had to realize my plan needed to change so I had to take action in a different direction. At that time I looked around and in May of 2012 it made a lot of sense for me to flip my sports nutrition store so I did.

One of the things I implemented in my sports nutrition store was I always do better than a win-win. I try to have a win-win-win. What I mean by that is I look for ways to create incentives. How can I have outside sales reps for me that work on commission? So I created an index card type flier with the store's information on it. At the very top it says "referred by." I would make thousands of them at a time. A map to the store was on the back, there were pictures of the supplements, it had out logo on it; those cards were really great. I'd hand them out and tell people they could get a discount if they gave out the fliers. They'd put their initials or name under the "referred by" section and they'd get a discount every time someone brought in one of their cards. Plus the person who brought in the card would get a free shaker cup and I'd help them with their supplements. That made it a triple win. That was just one of the actions I took. Another action step I took that really turned

things around for that store was I started doing free nutritional seminars at yoga and pilates studios, gyms, MMA studios, large gyms really just about everywhere. I would go in and give a discount to the owners and trainers and they'd give out free samples and meal plans and I'd do a half hour seminar with Q & A. I just kept taking that action. We'd set up booths with samples at gym openings. Across the street was a hand-wash car wash and I'd have guys setting up tables and giving out samples on Saturdays. People would come across the street and into the store. Again, taking that action brought those people and circumstances into my life that brought about positive changes. We became the "go to" store in the north county San Diego area. Again, in 2012 it just made a lot of sense to flip it because I had enough equity and saw how the industry was going.

For about year after I sold that business I took time off. I was just trying to figure out what the next business I wanted to get into was. I started dabbling in online businesses with programs and products but things just didn't feel like they were clicking for me at that time. So I put all of that on hold and I opened up a fire restoration business out here in San Diego. It had been just about a year from when I sold the store. Now again, I knew no one in that industry out here in southern California but I started taking action. I put a game plan together. I reached out to all the industries I knew that could feed me work. I googled and made lists and created spread sheets and I called and cold-called all day long. I made notes and put those notes into spreadsheets and kept calling for about two months straight. I kept hitting it every single day. I followed up and drove to those offices to introduce myself and hand out cards. Again, it was taking action.

After about two months things weren't really clicking so I asked myself what else I could do. I thought maybe I'd turn in a different direction. Well, because I'd had experience back east with fire restoration I knew there was a different avenue but because I didn't really know anyone in that industry in southern California I didn't really have those contacts. I knew the only way to get those contacts or go out and meet those people was to go out and take action. I knew there was another way to get business because fire restoration companies often work for insurance companies because we handle smoke and fire or water damaged properties. I knew there were services out there I could sign up for that would give me leads. So I signed up and got those leads and hit the street hard for months at a time.

There were two things that came out of that experience. The first was I had started meeting contractors and adjusters I knew could give me work right there on the spot. So I had my meetings face to face. I could also go in and solicit for business and potentially make money. Two or three months of doing nothing but that combined with following up with phone calls from my spread sheet ended up with me meeting exactly the right people at exactly the right time. All because I took that action business started coming in. Towards the end of 2013 I was starting to really roll and get that momentum.

In 2014 we crushed it and I'll give you an example. I hit the same numbers in 2014 after about a year and half with the business out here that it took me and my business partner back east about six years to hit. The same monthly gross numbers! I did that because I took that intensive, massive action on a consistent basis. And I'd met the right people at the right time who fed me work. Before I knew it business was absolutely booming in 2014 because I just kept moving forward. I had to adjust and figure out why the first things I did weren't working, I had to look at what I could add to my plan or what I needed to do differently but I kept moving forward, I kept taking that action. I started running fires, meeting people, creating relationships. Dinner meetings, lunch meetings, phone conversations, cold calling offices, walking into offices and introducing myself and handing out cards, whatever it took to get in front of the right people all on a consistent basis. It all goes back to perspiration. It all goes back to action.

So many people are so afraid to be wrong they're so afraid they're not perfect. You can't worry about that. If your goal, your destination is big enough you're not going to worry about how it's getting done anyway. The only way you're going to know is to keep moving forward, as you move forward it's going to unfold. You also need to have the wherewithal and common sense to take a step back and realize when something isn't working and make changes when you have to make changes. Or if you need to add something in like I did after those first two months of cold calling and spread sheets. I realized that by itself wasn't going to get me where I wanted to go so I needed to figure out what else I needed to do.

I've always kind of had that DNA I'm much more of an action taker than I am a planner. Sometimes that does come back and bite me when I don't think things all the way through but because I have such a strong will for action I'll just sort of will myself through the bad times. I just outwork some of those bad times. Now I know that's not in everyone's DNA but if you don't have that action oriented DNA you either need to figure out how to find it yesterday or you might want to rethink being a full time entrepreneur. Or you could partner with someone who has that drive, that determination, that entrepreneur DNA. Someone who isn't afraid to fall down. Plus if you're someone who can keep things together on the back end, the filing, the books, the phone calls that's a great marriage then because most entrepreneurs aren't the best when they are sitting in the office. I know I'm not my best when I'm sitting in my office all day when I have to do the estimates or the paperwork or the books. I have people who do those things for me know because

I know I have to run with my strengths and enhance my weaknesses. My strengths are action oriented.

So let's recap a little bit. If you don't already have this action oriented DNA it could still be ok if you're willing to take some action and find an action oriented partner you can resonate with. Find someone you can really connect with first and foremost, but then make sure they really have the skills, the DNA that's going to enhance your weaknesses. You don't want a partner that does the same thing you do, you're just not going to get anywhere. If you don't have something in your DNA look for a partner who does have it first or maybe you need to find that action DNA in yourself. Maybe you just need to dig deep enough, maybe your why needs to be bigger to make you take that action. I'm not saying there is no alternative, just that those are the two alternatives that come to me.

I do that whenever I get into a business. I look for whoever is going to enhance my weaknesses, who is going to fill the void so I can use all my energy on my strengths. I want to run like crazy with my strengths and not get so consumed with my weaknesses. I think that's what stops people as well, they get so consumed with what they can't do that it's all they focus on and they forget about what they can do. That's part of a business plan whether you put it down in writing or it's in your head. You have to put down what your strengths and weaknesses are.

That comes back to your level of awareness. As an entrepreneur your level of awareness needs to increase every single day. That should be top on your list. Then as you're growing your level of awareness in your people as a leader has to be second to none. That's an art that needs to be sharpened every single day in order for you to keep moving forward, growing and expanding. Action is everything. I know I've talked about this before, the trifecta in business and in life is inspiration, motivation and perspiration. You can have the greatest motivation in the world and you can have the biggest why or inspiration you could ever come across but if you're not willing to take that action it's just not going to happen.

Again action is everything. If you're not going to take the action figure out a whole other alternative whether that's partnering with someone or just not being an entrepreneur. Understand it's ok if you don't have that entrepreneurial DNA. There are also different types of entrepreneurs, A, B, and C right, but you have to be honest with yourself so you can move forward in a good solid direction. Remember action is fear's kryptonite so when that fear barrier starts creeping in just take action.

I'll give you another tidbit that completely works for me. I'm motion oriented, meaning I think the best when I'm at the gym or walking or even driving. I really do think the best when I'm in motion. Now that's not true for everybody but figure out how you work the best. Some people go to yoga, that's their zen. My zen is the gym. Figure out what that is for you so you can keep taking action and moving forward. Understand as you're thinking about this, just start doing it. Then all of a sudden it's just going to unfold.

I'll give you a little visual on this. Let's just say you had to walk to work, that's your commute. You had to walk from your house to your office and let's just say to do that you had to walk through a corn field. See yourself walking through this corn field. When you start walking through this corn field and you picture those big corn stalks, six, seven feet high, you keep walking and what's going to happen? You might trip, you might bump into corn stalks, or you might have to go around them or weave through them. After a while you're going to start to beat a path down. After a while that path is going to be much, much smoother.

That's exactly what happens when you start taking that action. It's going to be tough and choppy and sometimes you're going to fall down, lose your balance maybe scrape your knee but you get back up, wipe yourself off and keep doing it. As you keep doing it it's going to get easier and easier as long as you keep paying attention and adjust accordingly. I wanted to give you that visual because we think in pictures. If I tell you not to think of a pink elephant what happens? A pink elephant runs across the screen of your mind.

So just think about this visual. You're walking across that corn field and after a few weeks, a few months, maybe even a few years you beat down a path you could probably drive a car through if you needed to. It started to become so familiar because you started to really own it and that's what taking action does. In the very beginning, man was it tough. I say this on social media, in my workshops and in my keynote. The bottom line is action makes you earn it and life decides the rules for all of us. Life says if you're not willing to earn it then you don't deserve it. If you are not willing to earn it, you do not deserve it. Action dictates every single thing that we do or that we don't do.

Next time you're thinking about something and you want to keep putting that game plan together remind yourself all you're doing is buying time so you don't have to go into that darkness. Remember that darkness is only temporary as long as you keep moving forward.

OK just one more visual here because I love this subject. You're going through a haunted house, it's dark, things are coming out of the woodwork and scaring you, you're screaming and you just want to get out of there. If you stop in the middle what's going to happen? It's going to be even worse. If you try and turn around and go back, same thing, it's going to be worse. What do you have to do? You have to keep moving forward. Even at a slow pace you're gaining and you're not standing still. Remember we're always doing one of two things in life, we're either moving forward or we're moving backward. When we're moving backward long enough we disappear. So keep moving forward. Take that action. Don't be afraid to fall down. As long as you're learning from it, just get back up, wipe yourself off and keep moving forward. Get back in that saddle.

You know guys I want to leave you with what is probably my favorite quote of all time. It's about action. "All that stands between you and the ride of a lifetime is simply getting in the saddle and seeing what you're made of." That's where I want to leave this chapter, so thanks guys!

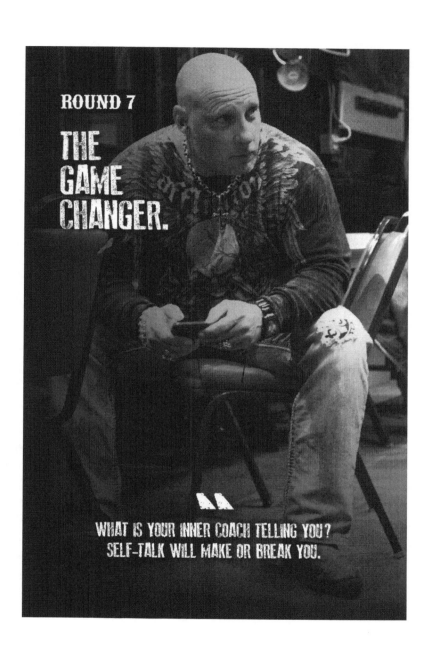

ROUND 7

THE GAME CHANGER.

WHAT IS YOUR INNER COACH TELLING YOU? SELF-TALK WILL MAKE OR BREAK YOU.

I call this chapter "The Game Changer in life" because it's the most under-utilized, misunderstood, misrepresented step in anything you might want to create in your life, personal, professional, physical or any other part. If you don't learn to understand and utilize this game changer a whole lot is not going to happen for you. I call this the game changer, but it's your self-talk your inner coach.

What are you telling yourself on a daily basis? Are you telling yourself things that are strengthening, empowering, uplifting or is it weakening, depleting and moving you backward? Most people, if they're honest and audit their day, will look back on their day and find it's depleting, weakening to them. Self talk like you're not smart enough or pretty enough or whatever enough is common and most people who haven't done a lot of self development fill their days with this negative self-talk.

We all have stories that we tell ourselves and a lot of these stories start when we're very, very young because self-talk ties in with the subconscious mind. Our mind is broken down into different sections. If you picture your mind as a circle and draw a horizontal line straight through the middle the top part of the circle is your conscious mind and the bottom part is your subconscious mind.

The conscious part of your mind can accept or reject anything. Things like you're a good person, or very loyal, or you're a great friend or partner. Or the reverse like you're a horrible person, you cheat, you lie and you steal. Again your conscious part of your mind can accept or reject any of this. When we're young it's completely wide open so we're accepting of what we're hearing and that then that gets impressed upon our subconscious mind. Our subconscious mind is omnipresent it's really in every single cell in our body. So the stories that we tell ourselves consistently really come from our conditioning, our subconscious mind. You can learn how to change this when you learn how to use powerful, positive self-talk.

Before I really get into how you go about that I want to say I do teach this in my corporate workshops, I really get pretty deep into this. Napoleon Hill, who I consider to be the godfather of personal development, wrote what I believe is probably one of the first books people picked up about personal development. That book was *Think and Grow Rich.* He's written other books, but to me this was kind of like the Holy Grail of personal development and mindset, how the mind the conscious and the subconscious and the body all work together.

In Chapter 4 of *Think and Grow Rich,* Napoleon Hill talks about auto-suggestion, which is what I call self-talk. Same exact thing, just different titles. Napoleon Hill said "Auto-suggestion is a term which applies to all suggestions, all self administered stimuli which reach one's mind through the five senses. Stated in another way, auto-suggestion is self suggestion." Now Napoleon Hill considers auto-suggestion as the most important part of his formula of getting rich. Understand *Think and Grow Rich* is not just about monetary gains it's about whatever area of your life you want to become rich in whether that's personal and/or professional relationships, your physical body, your spiritual health, really whatever matters most to you. That's really what personal development is.

Also in Chapter 4 of *Think and Grow Rich*, Napoleon Hill says "you are now reading the chapter which represents the keystone of the arch of philosophy. The instructions contained in this chapter must be understood and applied with persistence if you want to succeed in transmuting desire into money."

Now that's the other thing I want to touch on when it comes to self-talk, see self-talk is no different if you just want to try and get in shape. If you want to try to get in shape you can't go to the gym once a week, once a month or once a year. Well you can't do that with self talk either if you want to change your conditioning and change your inner coach. Understand all of that negative conditioning didn't happen overnight so changing that into a positive conditioning isn't going to happen overnight either. You didn't become out of shape, overweight, become weak physically overnight it took time, so you're not going to get in shape, get stronger and more vibrant overnight either.

This is a process. Self-development is a process and it needs to be applied every single minute that you can during every single day. Fill your whole world with personal development that resonates with you. Obviously Napoleon Hill, Dale Carnegie, James Allen and several other personal development authors, they all started everything for me. They got me going the right direction in personal development.

So, self talk, how do you really utilize it on a consistent basis? I had a mentor about 12 years ago who referred me to a book. You know, you here this all the time, "this changed my life," but I'm going to tell you this book literally changed my life. It changed my life to the point where the things I learned in this book from this author I have used every single day since I was introduced to them. Now before I get into this let me share with you that about 15 years ago I was introduced to positive affirmations and the power of auto-suggestion not only by Napoleon Hill but by Bob Proctor. For those of you who don't know, Bob Proctor's whole training is based around Napoleon Hill's teachings, especially the book "Think and Grow Rich" in fact he still carries around his copy he bought back in 1962. I've had the opportunity to see that book and it's all taped up and has seen much better days but he still keeps it with him.

Now Bob used to teach, and he taught me, something called the goal card. The way it works is you write down whatever it is you want on a card and put it in your pocket then take it out and read it throughout your day. He also taught us how to actually word that card. I started to do this and for a few years I kept my card in my pocket, I'd take it out and read it throughout the day and it definitely made a difference but when I was introduced to this man, Dr. Shad Helmstetter, and his book "What to Say When Your Talk to Yourself" it actually changed my life.

I'll tell you why, it's because the things he teaches are complete auto-suggestion. Meaning, that affirmation you write down that goal you write down, he takes it a step farther. Dr. Shad Helmstetter understood our subconscious mind is so powerful that if we record what we want in a certain way and listen to it throughout our day no matter what we're doing our subconscious mind takes it in. You can do this in the morning when you're getting ready for work you can just put that recorder on and listen while you're doing everything else you need to do. It doesn't matter if you're sitting there completely focused on listening or not, your subconscious mind is still taking it all in. Dr. Shad Helmstetter shared that you need to word it a certain way you need to own it however you word it and you need a start and end date. That's your road map. Now your conscious and your subconscious can work together.

One of the stories he shared in this book really grabbed me from the moment I read it. I share this story a lot of the time when I do my keynotes and in my workshops because it really was so powerful to me. This book was written back in the 80's and it was a little soft-back book. If you looked at this book in a store like Barnes & Noble you'd say "what's the big deal?" Nothing jumps out at you nothing looks impressive about this book. But man, when you open this book and start reading the pages it is so powerful, then when you start to apply the formulas the things he teaches, it takes everything to a whole other level.

So this story he shared from back in the 80's was he wanted to lose 60 pounds in 90 days. He put this affirmation together and recorded it on a little cassette recorder (remember this was this 80's). He would listen to it every morning while he and his wife were getting ready for work again at some point during the day at his office and finally every night when he and his wife were getting ready for bed. The 90 days hit and he got on the scale and he'd met his goal, he lost 60 pounds. The most interesting thing about this story is that his wife who had never gone on a diet lost over 20 pounds.

When I first heard this story it just blew me away but when I think about it and analyze it and break it down it makes a lot of sense. It really does because our subconscious is so powerful, it's omnipresent, it's in every cell in our bodies. Our mind is in every cell of our body; don't get it confused with the brain. You know they have Albert Einstein's brain in a jar in Rutgers, New Jersey, and the last I heard it's just sitting in the jar. See, the brain without everything else is just a mass, it's just an organ. Our mind is omnipresent; it's in every single cell in the body.

That's why energy is the most powerful force in our universe. That's why you can walk into a room and right away feel the energy if you're tuned in-either positive or negative energy. You can meet someone for the first time and realize you really connect with that person on an amazing level or that there's something about that person you really don't "feel" at all. That's our intuition, our gut feeling I call it our energy ps that all ties into the mindset to the omnipresent to every cell in our body to how we're built. This is why we can create self talk that's so powerful, how we can create such a powerful inner coach.

When you're writing down these affirmations, these goals, those things you want to accomplish the first thing you need to understand are the most powerful words in our vocabulary.

Those words are "I am." Now "I am" is a double-edged sword it can be our best friend and take us places we never thought we could go or it can be worst enemy and our heaviest anchor if we can't identify and cut loose from that anchor. What I mean by that is "I am a great person I am very loyal I am very honest I am a hard working individual." Then you own that. But there's also a reverse "I am a bad person I never follow through on what I say I'm going to do I tend to be dishonest." How does that resonate with you? What do you start to tell yourself? You own it either way. I am becomes ownership of whatever it is you tell yourself.

One of the things Bob Proctor taught me when writing down goal cards was to take it a step further. Start it off with "I am so happy and grateful now that." That encompasses everything under one roof. "I am" the most powerful words in our vocabulary with "happy," which we all want to be happy, and "grateful." The attitude of gratitude is the most powerful force to turn any negative around into a positive because it's impossible for us to focus on two different avenues, two different levels at once. Meaning if I'm grateful, if I'm in that attitude of gratitude it's impossible for me to be angry or upset at that same moment. Now if you let that attitude of gratitude go and focus on being negative, being angry or being a victim then you don't have any room for gratitude. It's only one or the other in that moment. The key is to stay in that moment. So use "I am so happy and grateful now that" in all your affirmations and definitely put a start and an end date.

Another thing that's really powerful when you word your affirmations, "I am so happy and grateful now that (whatever that is for you) on or before your end date. By doing that you're telling your subconscious is that whatever you want could happen before your end date or on your end date. Again, you own it all the way through. How you word this is so vitally important.

Here's what happens, when you start to implement this on a daily basis continuously you start to change your whole conditioning. You start to find yourself wording things in that way throughout your day. What that is telling you is you're starting to create a shift, a movement, a forward positive motion in your old conditioning. You're starting to create positive conditioning and the only way to do that is through self talk and understanding this process. Understand something too since I was introduced to this 12 years ago I've never stopped doing this. These days I sometimes have three or four recorded affirmations on my phone at one time. I listen in the morning when I get up, when I'm working out, sometime during the day, and always right before bed. Here's why it's important to listen right before you go to bed, when you go to sleep your subconscious mind is open like a sponge that's why if you watch a scary movie right before bed a lot of the time you're going to have nightmares. You want to fill your subconscious with positive reinforcement and you can't get a better result from a positive affirmation than something you wrote down that you want to obtain on or before that certain date.

Here's where else it's so powerful -recording your affirmations in your own voice. Let's break this down. You have the verbiage, the wording that you're going to own with an on or before actual date. Now you've drawn a line in the sand and created a road map. Taking it a whole other level now you've recorded it and you're listening to it in your own voice. So you're owning it in both text and in audio forms. This is so, so powerful. Here's the other beautiful thing, it doesn't have to be only goal related, you can write down and record affirmations that just increase your self-image. You can use this process to increase and build whatever you want to increase and build inside yourself. You can write down the most amazing affirmations and quotes that are going to help build you as a person from the inside out.

That's really what personal development is. It all has to start from the inside, only then can the outside start to change. The only way you can do that is through self talk, auto suggestion, there's just no other way. Self talk is our biggest "stopper" or our biggest catapult. You decide which one. You decide which way you go. You can go in a positive direction especially when you implement some of the things I've shared in this chapter, in this round. How you use self talk makes all the difference in the world and that's what I wanted to share in this chapter.

It's good to have more than one or two sentences on your card, it's a little bit longer and that lets you really own it, start to really take it in. So my suggestion is maybe three, four, maybe even five sentences if you can. If you can't, it's still better to do one or two sentences than not to do it at all. Ideally though if you can start off "I'm so happy and grateful now that..." and have maybe four or five sentences with "on or before" if it's an actual goal. End with some sort of a positive, I always end mine with "I want to thank the universe." I believe that the universe can become our best friend or worst enemy, but we're the ones who make that decision.

Who we are, what we want and what we get all start with either positive or negative self talk. Here's another thing you'll want to try if you're a parent, grand-parent, older sibling, aunt or uncle and you really want to start making a difference in a little person's life. Start telling them how proud you are of them, how amazing they are and all kinds of other good things. Start feeding that good stuff into their subconscious. Even if you have a kid who's a troubled kid, if you start to do this on a consistent basis they start to own the positive stuff just like they did the negative. Who you hang around with you become, why is that? It's because your subconscious takes it in. It becomes part of your identity, a part of your self talk. So if you want to see a difference in your kids start to pay attention to what you tell them because that becomes their conditioning, which becomes their auto suggestion and their self talk. If you want to take it a step farther, teach them how to do this on their own. Teach them how to put together an affirmation that's positive and uplifting and powerful then teach them how to listen to it throughout their day.

Really today everyone, even kids, have smart phones and if you have a smart phone you have a hand-held recorder right at your disposal whenever you want it. Put your ear phones in and listen to it over and over and over and just feed your subconscious mind. What you feed your subconscious is what you become. What you feed grows. Feed that powerful positive self talk and watch it grow.

This is an absolutely game changer, an absolute life changing process. For Napoleon Hill to say auto suggestion is the nucleus of everything you want in your life, well to me that says it all because he really was the godfather of personal development in my opinion. So think about this, start to implement it and let me know how you start to feel. If you apply affirmations on a consistent basis for 45 days straight I promise you will start to see a change in everything.

Here's what it does. Everything here is a double-edged sword, that's how powerful our minds are. Whether you become better or worse is completely dictated by your own mindset. For example, if you want into a gym and you don't really love the gym, it's really not your thing you're probably going to have self talk like "everyone's looking at me, I feel self conscious, I don't belong here etc." What do you think your state of mind's going to be? It's going to be in the gutter. All because of that self talk, that auto suggestion. Now let's flip that around. What if instead your self talk was "I love going to the gym, the gym's my iron therapy, if I didn't have the gym I wouldn't know what to do with myself, I always leave the gym with a clear head." Think about that state of mind. Think about that state of being. Which would you rather be?

It all starts solely with auto suggestion and self talk. I can't say it enough, I can't drive this home enough self talk is the nucleus of anything and everything you want good or bad. The problem is when you look back at your day or week honestly and you audit that day or week I promise you unless you implement these steps you're going to look back and find it was depleting, weakening most of the time. You're going to be blown away by all the negative stuff you tell yourself which creates your mindset which creates your reality.

Understand everything starts with your thoughts with your self talk, your auto suggestion. Pay attention to what you're telling yourself because you are listening!

ROUND 8

YOU CAN'T OUTPERFORM IT.

>> YOUR SELF-IMAGE CAN BE BUILT UP, TORE DOWN, IT JUST CAN'T BE OUTPERFORMED.

This is my favorite subject in personal development, your self-image! The reason self image is my favorite subject in personal development is because I believe that everything starts and stops with your self-image. I believe your results are dictated by the level of your self-image and I also believe you can build your self-image up or tear it down but you cannot outperform it. Let me repeat that because it's so vital to understand. You can build up your self-image or you can tear down your self-image but it is impossible to outperform it. So whatever your self-image is at is going to dictate the direction you go in life and the results you get. Everything, everything, everything you get in life follows your self-image.

I believe that's how powerful our self-image is because it's tied in directly with our conscious and subconscious mind which we talked about in earlier chapters how your subconscious mind is omnipresent and in every cell of your body. Now I want to talk about how powerful our self-image can be, either good or bad. See it's all tied with the previous chapter, The Game Changer, those stories we've told ourselves, our conditioning. It's all tied in together, the stories we tell ourselves, our self talk, our conditioning, dictates our self-image and whether it's good or bad. When your self-image is not good or when it's weak you're just never going to be able to get the results you really want in life. You cannot outperform your self-image.

You can learn how to build your self-image up. You can learn to build a very powerful positive self-image just like you learned your self talk. But, if you don't know where you're at to begin with you have no starting point. Before we get in to that, I want to say to parents out there how important it is to build up your child's self-image. You know when your kids are small they take everything in, good or bad, they're like sponges. Remember my story is I was left back in the second grade, diagnosed with ADD, they said I had a learning disorder, and I never graduated high school. So my conditioning and my self-image when it came to academics and learning was in the gutter because I couldn't learn the way they wanted me to. I listened to what they said; I thought I just wasn't smart. I loved being outside and being physical because my self-image was much higher then, I was good at that. I was comfortable in that setting.

I really struggled in that classroom setting so I always had tutors, sometimes in a group and sometimes one on one. That's where I really excelled academically because I wasn't distracted and wasn't in that classroom setting. I could focus and really stay with that teacher, that tutor, and that's when I learned the best. Obviously you can't do that all the time in a traditional public school system. Going back to self-image though, when I was 19 I found myself in a jail cell looking at major time, 8 to 10 years if things didn't go right. That all goes right back to my self-image and what I believed about myself and what you believe about yourself is what you start to act out. You start to move in that direction.

I believe that life is pretty simple but it's not always easy. Your thoughts, your feelings and your actions will always create your results. Think about that. The thoughts that you think create the feelings that you feel and the actions you take which creates the results that you get good or bad. You can turn that around. You can go back to the top and reevaluate what you're thinking and what you're feeling and those actions you're taking so you can get different results. All of that boils down to your self-image what you think about yourself, what you feel about yourself physically, mentally, and spiritually. All of it ties in together.

Another thing that will enhance your self-image, actually make or break you especially when you're younger is who you surround yourself with. My story was I wasn't supposed to win I wasn't smart I wasn't supposed to do well in life. I wasn't supposed to expect a lot out of myself when I became an adult.

That's what I heard so that's what I expected. My early years were a real struggle up until about my early 20's. I took certain action because of my circumstances and a person came into my life that showed me there really is something else out there. Only if you're willing to work, willing to get dirty and fall down then get back up again and stay out of your comfort zone there's a whole other world out there. He showed me all of that and I ran with it.

Luckily for me I've always had a really strong work ethic. I tie that in with seeing a whole other world I had never been exposed to because I was in that little cookie cutter mode all of those years. When I left school, didn't graduate high school, and then struggled for a few more years I attracted this individual into my life. I say attracted because I believe we attract those people and circumstances good or bad into our lives by the thoughts we think the feelings we feel and the actions we take. So I attracted this person into my life.

Now I couldn't identify it then but I certainly can identify it now that person showed me a whole other direction and I never looked back. Before then I was just a laborer in construction because I was a physical guy and I thought that's all I could do. I was that circus elephant - remember how they train baby elephants by tying a rope around its back leg that's attached to a stake in the ground? The baby elephant grows up not thinking it can move around because it's tied in one spot. So when it's a grown elephant and could easily break free it still stays right there because its conditioning reminds it that it can't go any further than the rope it stays in that little radius. I was that elephant. In reality that grown adult elephant could just rip that stake right out of the ground any time it wants. So I needed someone to show me I could tear that stake out of the ground. Prior to that I never thought I could. All I ever thought I could ever be was a laborer in construction. But because that person came into my life and because I took action because I was willing to stay outside of my comfort zone long enough to learn a whole other part of the world I never looked back. Before I started my first business I was in straight 100% commission jobs. If I didn't bring it in, I didn't eat but that worked really well for me.

I didn't know it then but looking back I have a real entrepreneurial DNA and that's why I didn't fit into that cookie cutter mold early in my life. I just don't "bloom" well in a confined structured environment. I need to be creative I need to be able to color outside the lines. That's where I work best and I'm able to be who I am in an industry that says otherwise. I don't look, act or talk like most motivational speakers, most inspirational speakers or even most authors. That's just not who I am. I had to learn it's OK to be who you really are. When you are who you really are you know your self image becomes bullet proof and doors open for you that you never thought possible.

You can't get there until you build on that self-image which is what I call becoming bullet proof in life. So that no matter what is thrown at you no matter what is said no matter what obstacles you have your self-image will pull you through because you know you'll be able to conquer it because of your self-image. This reminds me of a quote by Mohammad Ali he said he always knew he was a champ before he was a champ. This was because in his mind he had that self talk that conditioning "I'm the greatest, I'm the greatest." Listen whatever you tell yourself consistently for a long enough period of time you're going to believe whether it's good or bad. He just happened to tell himself such great things about himself that he started to become that started to believe that. Then those actions and the results all coincided with that inner belief he created from all those great things he said about himself to himself. Self image will absolutely start or stop your whole world.

Understand as you're building that self-image and breaking through those fear barriers and as you're crushing those obstacles what's happening is you're becoming that person you need to become to obtain your goals and hold onto them. It's not just about obtaining the goals you have to become that person you need to be to get and hold onto those goals. Most people talk about financial goals they have certain financial goals they want to achieve. In order to obtain that they have to build a strong enough self-image to become that person. But if you don't keep building that success you achieved either monetarily or physically or spiritually starts to go away because you don't keep growing into that person to keep it.

I'll give you an example. I think the last I heard the statistics were 75% or 80% of people that win the lottery that had never had money before will lose it within two years no matter what the amount they won. Think about why that is. How can it be that someone can win millions of dollars and even tens or hundreds of millions of dollars and can lose all of that money within two years? It's because their self-image will not allow them to keep it. See they didn't become the person who could hold onto that money. Probably the biggest factor is they didn't earn it and in order to build your self image, in order to become stronger you have to get through obstacles.

Life makes you earn it and life makes the rules. Earning it means to become the person you need to become in order to obtain that goal. Where some people fall off is when they don't realize they've got to keep building. Once you reach that goal you've got to keep going. If you stop once you reach your goal, well you're either moving forward or backward in life and if you stop moving forward you'll start moving backward. Like I've said before if you move backward long enough you disappear.

That's why those lottery winners cannot hold on to that money they won, it's going to be gone. That's exactly why successful people can lose everything then rebuild it very quickly their self image allows them to do exactly that.

I'll use Donald Trump as an example because pretty much everyone who reads this book is going to know who he is. He's a multi-millionaire maybe billionaire right? He just about lost everything and had multiple bankruptcies but rebuilt and not only did he rebuild but he rebuilt ten times over what he lost because his self-image allows him to do that. That's why if you look back through history and if you get behind the curtain of so many successful people you see that without their failures they wouldn't have had their success. But they wouldn't have been able to get through and learn from those failures without a powerful self-image.

One of the ways you know if someone has a powerful self-image and has that championship mindset is the look at life one way, they meet life head on, and they own every single thing good or bad. The pretenders in life are those people who say they have this or say they have that or they want this or they want that but they are always the victim. It's always somebody else's fault. When you hear someone talking like that you know they're going nowhere in life. When you can own what you did wrong learn from it and move on it will build your self-image. There is nothing that will build you quicker or stronger than life's lessons! I a big believe in this!

Don't even come at me with theory, theory is just going to waste my time and it will waste your time. Come at me with real wisdom from real life experiences because that's how I'm going to learn and that's how you're going to learn. We learn from real life, real world, experience and wisdom. If you aren't sure about that think about this. If you want to build a business and you've never built a business or you want to go into an industry that you've never been in before and you sit down with an experienced person who has been down that road and you listen to their advice and you listen to their wisdom there's nothing in a book you're going to be able to read or in a class you can take that will trump that because they've been down that road.

I'll give you another thing to think about when it comes to self-image and tying in wisdom with that because they're so interlocked. Let's say you're going to have major heart surgery tomorrow and you've got the choice of two doctors. Now the first doctor has been doing heart surgery for 20 to 25 years but this doctor didn't get their degree from a major medical school and they didn't graduate top of their class. The other doctor just graduated from one of the top medical school in the country and was at the top of their class but this doctor never had real world experience. Which one do you want operating on you? I guarantee it's going to be the doctor who's been doing surgery for the last 20 to 25 years because the things they've had to get through in the real world trumps the classroom learning every single time and trumps the controlled environment every single time.

Nothing trumps real world wisdom and I tie that in with self-image because at the end of the day that doctor couldn't get to where they're at without building their self-image along the way. They've created their self-image to know that whatever comes their way they're going to be able to figure it out and they're going to be able to handle it. That ties right in with entrepreneurs. Listen you might as well call entrepreneurs fire fighters right? We wake up every day and we just don't know what's going to come at us. We don't know what fires we're going to have to put out or what obstacles are going to be thrown at us. Not only that but no one is writing our checks for us. If we don't bring it in we don't eat.

Being an entrepreneur is one of the hardest jobs in the world but it's the most rewarding if it's in your DNA. If it's really how you're made and how you're built. Without building your self-image though nothing is going to happen for you. Always keep in mind it's about that person you need to become so keep building your self-image so you become that bullet-proof shield you need to keep moving forward as those obstacles, those fear barriers are being thrown your way. In a later chapter I'm going to actually break down how your self-image is actually built or torn down on a consistent basis and this ties in with every single piece of your life.

I want to give you another example from a very successful and well-known person, Oprah Winfrey. Now I want you to think about this, your self-image on all four pillars of your life could be different it could be stronger or it could be weaker. In your physical world if you're an athlete and you know how to get yourself in shape and you can stay in shape and you pride yourself on that then your self-image when it comes to your physical world is going to be very high, very strong. On the flip side if you're constantly struggling with your weight or if you're constantly struggling with getting into shape and staying in shape and making that lifestyle change your self-image when it comes to your physical life is going to be pretty low. If you're a very successful entrepreneur or business owner your self-image in business is going to be very strong because you've conquered so many obstacles and you've won more times than you've lost.

Now think about Oprah Winfrey. She is so outrageously successful monetarily, spiritually, emotionally when it comes to so many aspects of her life especially when you understand where she came from. She was a poor black girl who society said was not attractive. She was physically and mentally and emotionally abused up until her teens and early 20s. Her life was a complete struggle. She had to build her self-image to get to where she is now. Spiritually, emotionally, well she didn't start out that way she had to build to become the person who could obtain that and her financial success. She did it. Still somewhere way back inside her there's a stopper that keeps her from getting into shape and staying in shape and conquering that physical barrier whatever that reason is. She might not even know what that reason is. Maybe she just hasn't had a chance to identify it. If you look at Oprah Winfrey you just can't get much more successful that she is in so many different areas of her life. But think about that physical self-image, it's still lagging way behind the rest of her life. Understand she has access to the best trainers, the best chefs, and can create anything else she wants because of her other success. There's no reasoning behind why she can't get into shape and stay in shape except for her self-image on that pillar of life.

So all four pillars of your life need to be focused on not just one. Spiritual, Emotional, Physical and Professional are the four pillars of life and they are our whole life. Understand there will be times in your life one or two of those pillars are going to lag behind the others. Really it's about keeping some sort of balance in life but all of it goes back to your self-image for each one of those pillars because if you can't start building on your self-image you can't outperform it and after a while you actually start to go backwards. That's why the most successful entrepreneurs are constantly testing themselves to get better and why the most successful athletes are constantly pushing themselves to get better. They know internally they have to keep getting better or else they're going to start getting worse.

That's why it's so difficult for a high-level athlete to retire, it's their whole identity their whole self-image. You know if you put Brett Favre on the football field he's in his world, but you take him out of that and he has to build his self-image in different areas of his life. Maybe he already did that before he retired. But, and I'm guessing here, if you take him off the football field and throw him into the business world he would probably have a pretty low self-image when it comes to business. He would have to build that sense of self-image when it came to business. It's always our choice there are always options.

I'm going to bring this right around full circle to kids. If you have kids, if you're around kids if you're a school teacher or coach or a parent or grandparent really pay attention to this chapter because it can make or break a little child or even a teenager, actually especially a teenager because of the hormones and uncertainty that are their whole world for such an extended period of time. It all boils down to the beginning stages of what that child is told about themselves. It's all what that child is told. I'll give you another great example of a successful well known person and that's Gary Vaynerchuk, Gary Vee. Now for you social media people out there you know who he is, if you don't know who he is just google Gary Vee.

This guy is an absolute phenom when it comes to businesses. He took his father's liquor store in New Jersey that was making 3 million dollars a year and took it to a 60 million dollar a year company within a four to five year period by using the internet when youtube first came out. Then seven years ago he started a business with his brother, Vayner Media, and within seven years and $250,000 of his own money took that business from being work zero dollars and having three employees to grossing over 100 million dollars having four locations and 600 employees world-wide. When you hear him in an interview he talks about how strong his self-image is when it comes to

business and the inner confidence he's had. He's said when he looks back at the very beginning stages it's because his mom always told him how special he was and how amazing he was no matter what he did. If he tied his shoes his mother would tell him she'd never seen anyone else tie shoes as well as he tied shoes. It's the simplest little things and that's what started to build his self-image and his self-confidence. Now some people might mistake that for cockiness but I always tell people there's a really big difference between cocky and confidence. Cocky comes from the outside and usually means you can't back it up kind of like a bully or like that peacock who just doesn't want you to see behind the curtain. Confidence comes from the inside and it's just something you absolutely know.

When you start to watch Gary Vee you see he's really got that unbelievable inner confidence and that's that bullet proof shield. It all goes back to his original conditioning when his mom told him he could do anything over and over again and 1000% believed in him and told him every single day. So what happened is that built his self-image. Now on the flip side is that kid is told over and over that he's dumb, not to expect a lot out of himself when he becomes an adult, you can't learn, you're not smart enough and you're never going to get anywhere in life what happens? You start to build a self-image that tells you that's who you are.

So parents, grandparents, coaches, teachers listen up and start to change that conditioning if it's negative in those kids because they're taking it in like a sponge. They're listening to everything you say and taking it as gospel and they'll start to believe it. That's going to start their conditioning and build their self-image or it's going to tear it down. Hopefully if they have a bad self-image they have the wherewithal to surround themselves with the right people who will start to build that self-image. That's why I believe personal development should be taught from day one in every single school whether it's public schooling, private schooling or home schooling. Personal development is everything when it comes to life, business, relationships, and also understand your self-image is like a muscle you can't work on your self-image once in a while and expect it to be strong. You can't not test your self-image and expect it to be strong. See you can't build lean muscle and get into shape once in a while. You can't build lean muscle and get into shape without resistance training, going through some stress because what happens is during the recovery stage you build a stronger more reliable muscle. It's the exact same thing that happens with your self-image. You have to test it all the time and build on it and understand you're going to have failures. Those failures become learning experiences instead of devastation as your self-image starts to build.

Another thing I want to mention here is again Donald Trump. Before the presidential stuff I saw a youtube video and he was giving a keynote speech at one of the major colleges I'm not sure which one. It was just a little clip but he was standing there and said to always, always, always believe in yourself, don't ever not believe in yourself. He went on to say you know I've been around the most intelligent people the smartest people. The people society tells us are the most intelligent and smartest people. He said he'd graduated from the Wharton School of Business with them and had just been around what society considers the most intelligent people. He said he's also been around the most successful business people and said if he stepped back and looked the majority of those successful business people were not the ones that graduated top of their classes. They weren't the ones society said were going to make it. He said the ones society said were supposed to make it didn't make it anywhere near the level they were supposed to because they were able to handle the problems and put out the fires that came their way, it crushed them. But the people that weren't supposed to make it because they'd started out on a tough road had to build that muscle of resilience; they had to figure out how to handle them as those problems came. Then they figured out how to handle bigger problems as they came at them.

What happened is they built their self-image to be able to take on more and more. Like Bruce Lee said, don't wish for an easier life wish to be a stronger person to handle that tougher life. So many people want to be successful but as soon as more and more gets put on their plate they complain they whine they cry and they turn away. They don't understand that's part of the deal. See if you want to get better, if you want to succeed, you better learn how to build that self-image so you can take more on that plate. So you can handle more.

Oprah Winfrey said when she retired from the Oprah Show and she started the OWN Network the first few years she was just like a fish out of water. She said it was so overwhelming and she underestimated what it would take to get the channel off the ground. There were times she wondered if she would quit. Obviously her self-image had been built so strong and she had the team around her to keep moving forward but for her to say she was overwhelmed that she just felt so out of sorts for a period of time in that new business tells you that she's willing to grow and expand. Those thoughts come into every one of our minds. The difference is do you have the self-image, do you have the wherewithal to keep moving forward? That's going to be the key in your success, personally, professionally, spiritually and physically. Learn where your self-image is and learn how to build your self-image up and keep building. Build that muscle so you can handle more weight keep taking on more resistance and so you can keep growing. You don't want to hear that final bell ring and have regrets and you're going to have regrets if you don't learn how to build that self-image and keep moving forward and keep testing yourself. I'll see you in the next chapter. Keep making it happen!

ROUND 9

THE BULLY BUSTER.

DDMM

FEAR IS A CANCER. IF YOU IGNORE IT, IT WILL SPREAD AND TAKE OVER. GOTTA CUT THE CANCER OUT.

We're finally at the point in this book with all the information I shared in the other rounds it's a part of personal development that's unfortunately overlooked by a lot of other people that share this type of information. You know you can share a lot of information and you can share a lot of content but unless you can put that together in real steps for real practical results to me it's not complete. If someone's going to share something with me I'm going to want to implement it as soon as I can. I'm a big believer that theory just gets in the way. I want real life, real results-driven action steps so I can start to implement it right away. If you don't have that mindset you need to figure out how to find it or realize that maybe being an entrepreneur isn't in your DNA.

To be completely honest with you as a business owner, and an entrepreneur, as a CEO everything falls back on you. If you can't learn how to have that mindset of "let's do it now" and not put things off it's going to be a really, really uphill battle to create success in whatever business you're in. That really has to be the mindset to be successful in anything first and foremost. That being said I want to share with you what I call the bully buster because I believe fears and your fear barriers are just bullies. If you keep letting them bully you back into safety those fears are just going to multiply, they're going to compound and get worse and worse just like a bully. If you let that bully take that lunch money from you every single day it's not going to stop if anything it's going to get worse that bully is going to try to bully you for more and more until you actually stop that bully in his tracks.

That's why I want share with you today this four step formula, my bully buster system. This is also the subject matter for my TEDex video. At the time of this writing I'm waiting to get the OK from TEDex Temecula and it looks like everything's on track, cross your fingers we should get some answers back about the same time this book is released. So the Bully Buster, what's it really about? How does it apply to your life? That's what I'm going to share with you in this round.

The first step in the Bully Buster is identifying your goal your destination. I always ask the same question when I'm talking to corporations or doing workshops or even if I'm just giving advice; does it have the dynamic duo? Does it scare you and excite you at the same time? We talked about this in Round 4, the difference between setting goals and achieving goals. First and foremost in this process is that you have to identify your goal and your destination. You need some sort of direction. To make it even more powerful and to make it much, much more effective it really has to have what I call the dynamic duo; it has to scare you and excite you at the same time. If it doesn't it's simply not big enough.

The second step in this formula is your "why." I know we talked about this a little more in-depth in Round 5. When your why becomes big enough it will pull you through those fear barriers. When your why becomes bigger than you, you become unstoppable. When you hit those road blocks when you hit those fear barriers when you hit those obstacles always, always, always lean on your why. Your why is what's going to pull you through those tough times, especially if you're a business owner or an entrepreneur because it's such a lonely road for the most part. Now people don't want to tell you that because they want to create this sort of "airy fairy" type of "just think about it and it's going to come" or "think about it and it's going to manifest" and there is a certain truth to that but there's also a lot of massive hard tough action that needs to be applied too!

Also understanding so you don't feel blind-sided when you're than entrepreneur and you have that idea everyone else thinks is crazy but it scares you and excited you at the same time that you're going to feel lonely. There will be plenty of times you're going to feel like you're in the dark, like you're that buoy in the ocean. You're by yourself and feeling like you're being pushed one way and pulled the other way. That's all normal and actually that's what you want to start to feel for a few reasons; that's how you know you're on the right track, you know it's big enough and you know if you keep moving forward that darkness is only temporary.

I want to make sure that I clarify, being an entrepreneur or being a CEO, having everything riding on your shoulders is one of the toughest jobs you'll ever have but if you see it through it's also one of the most rewarding. Identifying and understanding and leaning on your why is absolutely crucial to success in anything in your life.

The third step is the action. What action are you taking and is it getting you closer to or farther away from your destination and your goal? I'm a big believer and we talked about this in Round 6, I'm a big believer that action becomes magical. As you start taking that action the people and circumstances start to come in to make it happen. That action starts to create results and understand results don't lie. Results are the greatest barometer we have in life because they don't lie. Results sometimes tell us what we don't want to hear as well as what we do want to hear but most importantly you are going to able to rely on your results because they are the most accurate barometer you can have and you can utilize them going through the darkness and going through tough times and hitting obstacles. Results always come directly from the action that's taken. Now if you're not happy with some of those results you just start changing course and we're going to get into that in a few minutes.

The last step which I call "The Game Changer" which we went into in Round 7 is your self-talk, your inner coach. What are you telling yourself? What is your team that you're leading, your organization, the division in your organization that you're leading? What are they telling themselves? Now think about this if you're a business owner and you have a sales staff and you have a customer service staff and they're telling themselves on a daily basis how bad it is or how the economy is not going to let them grow, how every customer that calls is a problem what do you think is going to start to manifest? It's going to be like a cancer that's going to start running through your whole business. So you have to learn and understand what you and your team are all telling yourselves on a daily basis. Then you can audit and start to change that self-talk before it becomes toxic. You want to catch it really early just like a cancer and cut it out. If not it's going to spread and kill everything around it.

Understand whether you have a 30,000 or more employee business or you're a one-person entrepreneur, solo-preneur, you are still the coach of your business. The self-talk, the action, the why, and the goals, the destination, all of it absolutely applies. It doesn't matter how big or how small that company is we are all vulnerable to these steps if we don't start to implement them on a consistent basis.

So again, Step 4 is your self-talk, what is it you are telling yourself on a daily basis and is it uplifting is it strengthening or weakening? Is your self-talking moving you forward or backwards? And as a leader you also need to identify that in your team whoever they are.

You can apply all of this into your personal life as well. If you are the leader of your family, even if you just live by yourself and you have no family members because remember you have to lead yourself first. In order to do that you have to know who you are and what you're telling yourself on a daily basis because then you can start to change it. If you don't know that it's broke you can't fix it. That leads us to the last bottom part of this formula which is your results.

Your results, your reality which becomes your self-image or if I'm talking to a company it becomes your coach of your business. Again, your results, your reality will not lie they're going to tell you the truth on the actions you're taking the people and circumstances that are coming into your life good or bad. Now that gives you something to actually work on and gives you something to change if needed. Here's the thing, when you break down this formula, The Bully Buster, maybe your goal does scare and excite you at the same time, maybe you're on track and maybe your why is big enough. Maybe your why is even bigger than you, but you're not taking that consistent action you need to take.

So when you look at this formula you can actually break it down into sections. If you're being honest with yourself and at the end of the day or end of the week or end of the months and you know you haven't taken that consistent positive action you should be taking or could be taking now you can narrow that down. You already know those other areas are in pretty good shape so you can focus and work on that action area because when you improve that one area that was lacking it makes all those other areas flourish. Everything else is going to be better it's like that saying "the better you make yourself the better everyone around you is going to be." That's important to understand.

You know you might have two areas in this four-step formula that are lacking or that you need to build on and the other two are pretty strong. Again it's going to be that same recipe with different ingredients. You focus on whatever that is, if it's your why and your action you need to figure out how to increase that why and make your why even more powerful and make it bigger than you plus take that consistent positive action. Maybe it's your self-talk and action. A lot of times people need to identify that their why is big enough and that their goal scares and excites them at the same time. Usually those are the two areas that need to be worked on the most on a consistent basis so you need consistent, precise, positive action. Do not be afraid to fall down and understand when you do fall down it's your greatest lesson in life and learn from it. Then stand up brush yourself off and move forward and don't look back.

Another area a lot of people fall down in is that self-talk, what is it that you're telling yourself? Why isn't your inner coach more positive and uplifting? Now you can identify that and start to change it. In Round 7 I gave much more information on self-talk and how to apply it on a daily basis. To be honest with you when you're not taking that consistent precise action I pretty much guarantee it's going to trickle down to your self-talk. It all works together all these areas have to be married at the hip.

Look at these are pillars, four pillars. As two or three pillars are really strong and holding everything up and you have that one pillar that's weak work on that one pillar. If you have two pillars that are really strong and powerful at that moment but the other two are lagging behind focus on those two weaker pillars so you can make them just as strong as or stronger than the others.

We think in pictures so I want you to think about this. Think about four legs of a table. If one of those legs becomes weak the table starts to rock. If two of those legs become weak the table starts to tilt. If three of those legs become weak the table just about tips over and if all four legs become weak that table is on its side or its back and it doesn't work at all. You're out. I wanted to give you a visual because we think in pictures. So think about you and your goals as that steady sturdy table that you always need to work on, always need to tweak, and need to figure out how to make those pillars even stronger.

Like we talked about earlier when you're going for that goal that scares and excites you at the same time it's not really about that goal believe it or not. It's about the person you need to become to obtain that goal, hold onto that goal and then move forward to another bigger goal and another destination that's going to keep making you grow and evolve. As we've talked about we're evolving beings that's why we're here. We are here to grow evolve and move forward. If we don't and we go back into safety we start to disappear everything weakens and starts to go away.

This formula will teach you not only how to identify and crush through those fear barriers and survive but it's actually going to teach you how to thrive. The only way to thrive is to keep moving forward growing and evolving. Happiness is completely tied in with fulfillment. That's how people can wonder how someone can be so unhappy when they have all this stuff and have created a lot of success in whatever area but most of the time we're talking about monetarily. It's because they don't feel fulfilled.

Fulfillment is tied directly in with happiness and the sooner you grasp that the sooner you can be happier in your life. That goal for that house or that car that bank account that relationship that physical body you want, whatever it is in your life, if it doesn't fulfill you and keep you fulfilled your happiness is going to disappear. It's going to start to dwindle. So this formula is directly tied in to your success more importantly to your fulfillment which is married to your happiness. At the end of the day I don't care who you are we all want to be happy. We all want to feel content and fulfilled. Even if we can't identify or define it that's truly what we want.

To me success really is living life on your terms and that's really married to fulfillment which as we've talked about is married to happiness. What good is monetary success if you're not happy? What good is success in a relationship if you're truly not happy and fulfilled? That's what you have to ask yourself so go back to this formula. Does it scare and excite you at the same time? Is it big enough is that why going to have enough juice to carry you through? What is the action you're taking on a consistent basis? Go back and audit these things, change them, tweak them and take that massive, massive action especially in the beginning because you have got to get that momentum. You've got to get that inspiration and there's no way to do that without perspiration.

Fourth step again is what is it you're telling yourself on a consistent daily basis? Only you can really be true to yourself. You know when it's dark the lights are out and you're by yourself whether or not you gave it everything you had that day or that week or that month. You are the one who has to live with it either way.

So go back to that formula, implement this on a daily basis and watch your whole world start to shift and start to change. The people that come into your life and the circumstances that happen will absolutely be amazing and it's going to floor you. There will be times you'll be absolutely in awe of all of it even when you know quantum physics tells us energy is things thoughts are things, what you think about comes about. All of that is great to remind yourself that you need to implement all of this in your life on a consistent basis to keep growing. But really life is going to smack you between the eyes in so many different ways good and bad.

Take this formula and run with it! Teach it to other people and help them move forward and crush through those fear barriers so they don't have to look back they keep moving forward and they keep growing and expanding. This is real life practical steps for real life practical results that has been utilized since the beginning of time. This just happens to be a formula I put together in my own way with my own flavor that works for me. Make no mistake this information goes back to antiquity. The information I've been taught has been taught to me and shared with me by some of the greatest mentors in the world and they were taught by some of the greatest mentors in the world. It keeps going on and on and back farther and farther through time to the beginning of time. So when someone says "how do you know if this works?" just look back through history. That's all you have to do. Again results don't lie.

So start to implement this into your life, this will teach you how to get that lunch money back from that bully and never be bullied again. Don't ever focus on surviving in life, always, always, always focus on thriving! We get one ride that I'm aware of and it's a really short ride even if we live a full life. So don't leave anything on the table, go get it, crush those fear barriers and teach others how to do it too. Pay it forward. That's really what we're here for as well, paying it forward, moving forward and don't look back.

I'm looking forward to when this book launches. I know I'm going to hear some great success stories that we can share, that you can share, because we're all in this together! Thanks and I'll see you in the next chapter.

ROUND 10

THE NEW UNDISPUTED CHAMP.

SOMETIMES ALL THAT STANDS BETWEEN YOU AND THE RIDE OF A LIFETIME IS SIMPLY GETTING IN THE SADDLE AND SEEING WHAT YOUR MADE OF.

Well it looks like you made it Round number 10! You went ten rounds with the Monster Motivator and I'm very proud you got to this point but to be honest with you, your work just started. You know this is a book with a lot of great information I've acquired over the years through hard work, dedication and also from some of the most amazing mentors. Like I mentioned in the beginning of this book nothing is theory it's all real world practical steps for real world practical results. I really do feel theory gets in the way and I have no time for theory let's just figure it out and move on. That's always been my M.O.

I called this round The New Undisputed Champ because if you follow this formula, if you follow this book, you will identify and crush through any of those fear barriers that come up. Some are going to be quicker some are going to take longer it all depends on how fast you learn, how fast you learn how to adapt and keep moving forward. That's going to determine how long you're stuck behind a fear barrier and how big of a goal you have. When you have a goal that scares and excites you at the same time it's a massive goal and it's a massive destination so in your mind you're going to have massive fear barriers.

In this chapter, this round, let's start at the top and work out way down. Round 1 is all about how it's not where you started but it is truly where you end up. More importantly than just where you end up is what you did in between your starting point and your destination. Meaning that in between part is your life it's your ride. So how was that? Even if you got to your destination but you hated the ride what good is that?

I believe that happiness comes from fulfillment and success comes when you're happy when you're excited and when you have that passion that keeps you up at night and wakes you up early in the morning. I tie that in with happiness. When you look at this in reverse, people always want to know what the secret to happiness is and it's fulfillment. What is the secret to success? Living life on your terms. They all intertwine, they all connect.

I wanted to share my story in this book because at this point in my life I was able to build and sell three companies in three different industries but it sure didn't start out that way. It took me 20-something years just to start to move in a positive more successful direction. Then another ten years to get to another level. So there is no overnight success, there is no magic pill, there is no magic formula that's going to give you the success you're looking for if you don't take action. There are a lot of little moving parts to this that you have to learn how to put together and change as you go. If you're not changing and your world is not changing and growing and evolving there's a trickle-down effect so nothing else will either.

So Round 1 is it's not where you started it's really where you end up but also it's that in between ride. When you look back how was that ride? When you're 80 or 90 years old if you're lucky to get to there healthy and you look back you should say "man that was some ride." If you can look back and say that, you've won, you've really won in life. If you look back and say "I wish I would have done that or why was I so scared of that" well my goal for this book is that you won't say that at all. My goal for you is that you never look back and have regrets because you left things on the table because you were too afraid to move forward. That's what so many people are, they're so afraid. Now you know what fear barriers are they're obstacles made up inside your head. So don't leave anything on the table, look back and say "that was an amazing ride." When you can do that you have absolutely won.

Getting into fear, we talked about that right? What is fear? Again it's that obstacle inside your head. It's that little, or even big, bump that depending on your perspective and depending on where you are in your life at that time. Understand fear barriers are just little tests they're just little boot camps life puts you through to see how bad you want it to see what you're made of and to see if you're able to become that person you need to become in order to obtain that goal and that destination.

Fear vs. Courage, we know that this whole concept and the whole thought process of being fearless is really getting you nowhere. A lot of the time it becomes frustrating. You're trying to figure this out, trying to figure out why you're not fearless. You think if you're not fearless you're never going to win. So you become frustrated and confused then what happens is you start to go back into safety because you don't think you can win. All because it's not an accurate statement to live by to say you need to be fearless. We all are going to have fear barriers. We're all going to have fear. It all depends on how badly you want to get out of your comfort zone on a consistent basis.

Who's that person you need to become in order to conquer that fear barrier, move on, grow, evolve and move forward? Now you know that courage is the key. Courage is that golden ticket. Courage means you're still afraid but you're also still moving forward through the fear. That's what true courage is. Remember that three-letter word "cor," that Latin word that means "comes from the inside." It comes from your heart, comes from your soul. That's where courage is manifested and it means it really means something to you, and because we are passionate and emotional beings that's what drives us. Learning how to have that passion and emotion work for you instead of against you is vital in learning how to identify and crush through those dreaded fear barriers.

We talked about goals right? You want to make sure you set your goals with that dynamic duo. Does it scare you and excite you at the same time? Remember again we are passionate and emotional beings and we work from feelings and when that feeling is so intense that it scares you and excites you at the same time you know it's big enough. Now you know that's the direction you need to figure out and keep moving forward.

You have to really, really, really lean on your why. When you hit that fear barrier and it's making you go back into safety and you feel like you're in that darkness you have to go back and lean on your why. Make sure your why is big enough and if that why can become bigger than you then you become unstoppable. Don't get consumed with the "how."

Action, nothing happens without action. You've got to be willing to sweat you've got to be willing to perspire. You've got to be willing to put a certain amount of sweat equity into that goal, into that destination and into your dream and into your life. If you're not willing to put sweat equity in you might as well stop now. There is no reason to move forward if you're not willing to lace up your boots get to work and make it happen. You have to be willing to fall down, get back up and wipe yourself off and keep moving forward and learn from it. The key is you have to learn from those failures, from falling down and getting back up because that creates wisdom. That wisdom creates a different person.

What are you telling yourself on a daily basis? What is your inner coach reminding you about? What's your inner story? We all have inner stories, what's the story you're telling yourself? Is it positive, is it strengthening? Is it moving you forward or is it moving you backwards? Is it depleting you and who you believe you are? Understand that once you've identified this you can start to work on it. You don't know how to fix something if you don't know it's broken. Your self-talk is going to be so vital to catapult you in the direction you need to go for that big scary dream or that big scary goal. This leads you to the epicenter, the bottom line which is your self-image. You can build it up or tear it down but you can not out-perform your self-image. Your self-image dictates everything you do or you don't do in your life. Your self-image is controlled by your self-talk and is controlled by the action you're taking or not taking. It's also controlled by your why and whether or not your why is big enough.

We went over the bully buster, the four-step formula, in chapter nine. That is a formula I promise you if you utilize it on a daily basis and you audit and are honest with yourself you will crush through any fear barrier that comes your way. As long as you're willing to apply it on a daily basis and always go back to it and re-evaluate. Always tweak it and figure out how you can make it better. That is how you're going to break through those fear barriers and trust me they are coming. Fear barriers will come like waves as long as you decide to keep moving forward and out of your comfort zone and growing and expanding. They'll come in wave after wave and you'll have to figure out how to make those waves work for you instead of working against you.

Looking back at my businesses and at my business life, I had so many different types of fear barriers. When I look back at my beginning fear barriers they were things like "I'm not smart enough" "I'm not supposed to be here" because I didn't do well in school. I was told not to expect a lot out of myself when I became an adult because I couldn't learn in a regular classroom setting. I was being judged by a certain criteria that didn't work with my DNA. That's just the bottom line, I'm not making excuses and it's not a victim mentality it just is what it is. I learn in a much different way, I'm a hands-on "appliable" learner and that's what I did in business.

My very first business was a public adjusting firm. I'd been an outside sales rep for years on 100% commission but I didn't know a lot about the back end of this business. There was so much I needed to know that I didn't know when I started but I didn't let that stop me. What I did was surround myself with people who did know those things I didn't know so that I could double-down and triple-down on my strengths. I was that front guy so I got out there and brought the business in while I made sure I had the right people in place that could do those things I didn't really know how to do or didn't do well.

I'll give you a great example. My office manager was someone I had hired from another company. She had been with another public adjusting firm for years when I made her an offer that she loved and she came on board. So then I had someone who knew the back end of the business. My business partner at the time we first started the company was the adjuster, he was the back end guy. I was the sales guy, I brought the work in. My partner wanted nothing to do with doing sales he wanted nothing to do with being out in the front. He wanted to be in the back and he was very good at that.

So when you have that fear of being not smart enough or of not having the experience or of not knowing enough take a step back for a second and take a deep breath and figure out who you can surround yourself with to keep making it happen. Remember what we talked about earlier, action is magical. When you keep moving forward the people and the circumstances start to come in.

If this is your first business or you've been in business and you're struggling or this is your fourth or fifth business but you want to approach it in a different way I always say reverse engineer it. Identify your weaknesses and enhance them with people or situations so you can run with your strengths. You know what your strengths are and you know what your weaknesses are by now. So surround yourself with those people who are strong in areas you are weak in.

I remember I watched an interview with Donald Trump a long time ago when he had just finished digging out from under a bankruptcy and all the craziness he went through in the 80's. If I had to guess I'd say this interview took place in the early 90's. The interviewer asked Donald Trump what the secret to his success was and how he was able to bounce back and not only bounce back but come back stronger than ever before. Trump didn't even blink an eye he just said it was all because of the people he surrounded himself with. He said he surrounded himself with the right people.

A lot of people don't know this but his casinos in Atlantic City went under not because of the economy, not because he's a bad business man, not because it was a bad business to get into because he did very, very well for a long period of time. It wasn't even the unions. What a lot of people don't realize is that his top three advisors in that casino business were all on a private plane that went down and they died. Once he lost his top three people he surrounded himself with that enhanced his weaknesses things started to crumble.

I read that he actually went over to Wynn casinos because they were friends. So he went to Steve Wynn and asked him what he should do and Steve Wynn told him to go to his casinos and figure out exactly what was going on and how to turn it around. He told Trump that he had to get his hands dirty and really get in there. What Donald Trump realized was he didn't really have the why he thought he had. His passion and his drive, the thing that gets his juices flowing is real estate, commercial real estate. Promoting, creating, even flipping commercial real estate is where his passion is. He's also a branding animal! This guy is just a branding beast. But he didn't have that same passion that same drive when it came to casinos. He just saw an opportunity as a business man surrounded himself with the right people and ran with it and did very well for a long period of time. When he lost those advisors in that plane crash everything crumbled because he couldn't replace them quick enough and he didn't have the passion and drive to turn it around himself. He absolutely had the ability there's no question about that. He also had the money but his why wasn't big enough.

I want you to think about that. I want you to think about how important it is that your why is big enough. He said he loves, he lives and he breathes real estate. I'm guessing someday he'll look back at his life and think he didn't leave it all on the table, he'll think about how he lived his life by his rules. When you can say that? Well it doesn't get any better than that. I believe that's what everyone should strive for.

The money the finances; that will come when you focus and stay consistent with what you want to do and what you love to do. Make no mistake just because you found something you love to do does not mean it's going to be easy. Also understand there is no better time than right now to be moving forward with your passion because of the internet, because of social media. You can become your own media platform. You can get to a point like a Gary Vee or a Grant Cardone where they've become their own media platforms and the actual traditional media now comes to them rather than the other way around. The internet has taken much of the leverage away from the traditional television stations. It takes a lot of the leverage away from Hollywood and it's moving more in that direction every single day.

So if you do have a passion don't get so consumed about how you're going to make money at it. Just start moving forward. Start taking that massive and consistent action. Then watch things unfold. Surround yourself with people that you know can pick up the slack and fill those gaps you might be leaving because they're not your strengths. Understand if it's done right and you're willing to put that hard work in you can become your own brand and you can become your own media platform. When you get your brand to a certain point it's over, now you have the majority of the leverage. That how people like Kim Kardashian can charge ten and even twenty thousand dollars just to send out a tweet - because her brand warrants that. Whether you like her or you don't and whether you agree with how she got there or not doesn't matter. Life doesn't care whether you like her or not. She created a brand and now she makes the rules. Now they come to her. Twenty years ago that didn't happen and thirty years ago it really couldn't happen.

Understand the world we're living in today, 2016 as of this writing, is showing that television is probably going to be going by the wayside just like radio did when television first started getting popular because of the internet. Everything is now on our phones. I'm sharing this with you because it's a perspective in business you have to understand. You have to learn how to identify the changes and really how to forecast the changes so that you can adapt. Like we mentioned earlier, you're either moving forward or you're moving backward and if you move backward long enough you're going to disappear. Again some examples of that would be Blockbuster Video, Borders Books and Kodak film just to name a few.

If you're not moving forward and if you're not staying on the cutting edge you are going to be obsolete and you are going to disappear. Gary Vee made a great point on one of his shows. He forecasts that in the next 15 to 20 years the amazons of the internet are going to completely crush the brick and mortar stores like the walmarts we have today because everything is going online. That's why Amazon is working on drone to drop off packages at your front door! They're playing way ahead of that curve.

Again this all goes back to identifying that major fear that we all have which is the fear of change. We get too concerned with trying to keep things the way they were. Life says evolution is inevitable. Life doesn't care whether or not you agree. Life doesn't care if you're ready or not. Life will not stop because of you.

When you completely understand that it completely changes the rules of the game. Now you just have to learn how to accept, adjust, adapt and move forward or you're going to be left behind. Understand the world you're living in. Understand the world you're going to be living in as best you can. Look at what will be happening over the next two, five, ten years so you can be prepared for the next change and so you can adapt to the next turn that comes down the road. Life is going to keep throwing turns in the road it's not a straight flat run. Life is a winding, bumpy road for a reason - life wants to know what you're made of. Can you handle it? Can you become that person you need to become in order to obtain your destination? That sounds simple but it isn't always easy.

In ending this book I want to thank everyone who supported me throughout the years. All of my mentors, friends, family members who all supported me at different times because I am such an entrepreneur at heart that when I moved in that direction a lot of those people thought I was crazy. Some of those people didn't start out supporting me they waited until they saw I was winning before I got their support and that's OK. Understand that a lot of time in your inner circle they're doing that because they are fearful for you they don't anything to happen to you. What they don't realize is they can't see what you see, they're not who you are, so keep reminding yourself they are not you and keep moving forward if it feels right inside.

If you have that little something inside that's tearing at you and pulling at you that only you can see. That's when you know you've got something to bite into. That ties in to your why. It's so vitally important that you stay focused on that thing inside you. That thing that's so crazy and so big no one else can see it except you especially in the early stages. When it has that dynamic duo that's what's going to happen, it only makes sense. If everyone could see it and everyone agreed and everyone said you absolutely could do it do you know what that tells you? It tells you it's not big enough. It tells you that you need to find something that's bigger or you need to add to it to make it bigger.

You get to a point as an entrepreneur, and I hope this book is going to help you move in that direction, where you actually start to look forward to that because you know if the masses are not agreeing with you you're moving in the right direction, as long as it feels right inside. Listen to your inner GPS. When you start to utilize that inner GPS it's just like a muscle - the more you use it the stronger it becomes and the more reliable it becomes. Just like a muscle the less you use it, the less resistance you give to it the weaker it becomes and the more unreliable it becomes. As a leader, as an entrepreneur, as a business owner, as a general manager even as a parent you have to learn how to listen and let your inner GPS guide you.

We were programmed with this as human beings and it's absolutely amazing. That's how you can walk into a room with a bunch of people and recognize there are one or two people who just rub you the wrong way. You don't even have to talk to them there's just something that doesn't feel right to you. Or vice versa, you met someone for the first time and you felt like you've known them forever. It's that inner GPS that intuition that gut feeling. It's vital to learn how to build up your inner GPS and make it strong a reliable so you know you can make those right choices move forward, build your confidence and feel like you have a strong self-image.

Everything and I mean everything that I've shared in this book was created by someone other than me. It all goes back to antiquity and it all works together. Every one of these rounds work together in one way or another they are all completely married to one another. Now the steps you use and how you use them depends on your situation or circumstance but I promise you if you rely on this book, if you go back to this book and read and re-read it, it will help pull you through. If you go back to a certain section or round in this book when you have a certain situation or circumstance, it will help pull you through. Now I can't say it "will" pull you through because you have to do the work but it will certainly help you if you do the work. I'm so confident that it will because it's not my information, I didn't create this. Again this all goes back to the beginning of time.

The only thing I'm doing in this book is sharing what has worked for me in the real world, what I was taught from my mentors in the real world, what I applied in the real world and I'm giving it all to you in my own flavor. The way I am. What you see is what you get with me so that's why this book is written this way. I'm as transparent as you can get and I believe that authenticity is a commodity. Authenticity is the commodity! You have to learn how to be true to yourself. You can't be true to yourself if you have a self-image that doesn't allow you to be true to yourself.

I want to thank you guys for investing in me, investing in yourself, and investing your time. Please don't just read this once, if you need to go back to it and read around here or there or wherever you need to read. Or reread this book over and over again. I promise you every time you read it and every time you read a section of it you're going to get something new. Not because it's so special and not because I wrote it a certain way and certainly not because I'm special. It's because you're raising your level of awareness and you didn't have that level of awareness the time you read it before. So nothing's changed in the book, it's just your level of awareness is rising so now you can get certain things you couldn't pick up before because you just weren't there. That's when you know you're growing. When you reread this and you realize you don't even remember reading something when you read it the first time or you get something you remember you didn't understand the first time. When you get to that point please don't stop, keep going and keep growing because that means you're winning and you're expanding and raising your level of awareness.

Now you're becoming that person you need to become in order to obtain that goal, that destination you're going toward. That's the key to all of this. That's why I wrote this book. I want you to keep raising your level of awareness keep growing keep expanding and to feel obligated to share the things you've learned with others. See this information doesn't work long-term if you keep it to yourself. You have to pay it forward. I promise you this. There aren't many promises I've made in this book but I do promise you this. Once you get to a certain level of awareness, once you start feeling like you can't get enough of personal development information, you can't help but share it.

You can't help but say this is what I've learned take what works for you and throw out the rest. That's just so vitally important, even with this book, take what works for you and throw out the rest. But I promise you if you go back and read it again and maybe even take notes or use a highlighter you will start to see your level of awareness grow. I'm hitting this point so hard because I want you to be able to identify when it starts to happen. If you can't identify it what good is it? You're not going to know. So I'm hitting this point because it's so vital and it's the reason I actually put this book together and I love sharing this information. I can't get enough of it. I'm always learning and I'm always listening to different motivational speakers. I know I can pick up new things from different people for different reasons. I also know there's not just one way to do this. You have to figure out your way. You have to figure out your DNA. You have to figure out how to enhance your own weaknesses and run with your strengths. You have to figure out your own level of awareness. Until you do all of that you can't lead others or even yourself effectively.

If you want to be successful in life and I don't care what area of your life that is, you have to become a leader. It doesn't matter if it's your personal, professional, spiritual or physical part of your life. There's not one successful person that you can think of either now or back throughout history to the beginning of time who was not a leader at some point in their life. Most were leaders at multiple times and in multiple areas of their life. If you can't be a leader of yourself and others there's no value. You're not bringing any value to the world or to your life. Life says if you're not going to bring any value you will not win long term. I don't make up the rules and you don't make up the rules. Life makes up the rules. So bring that value, raise your level of awareness, lean on that why, and move forward through that darkness. Understand that darkness is only temporary if you keep moving forward. It becomes permanent when you go back into safety.

Thank you guys so much! I hope you'll give me some feedback on this book and I hope you follow this through so you can learn how to identify and crush those dreaded fear barriers every single time!

Dave Daley, The Monster Motivator

Keep Makin' it Happen!

The Birth Of MMTV

I have been an entrepreneur my whole adult life....I have such a deep rooted passion for watching & helping other entrepreneurs knock out their dreaded fear barriers and move towards their dreams & destinations

I completely understand how it feels to be a full time entrepreneur ...it's a dark lonely road at times & if you don't surround yourself with a supporting cast...It's very easy to turn around back into safety

MMTV is a platform that created a very powerful Triple Win! The guest breaks through fear barriers shares their story & promotes their business, the Audience get behind the black curtain of the guest & takes in tremendous value from real word experience...nothing's theory on MMTV...they also have an opportunity to ask questions & interact live and stay connected with the guest after via FB.

I receive huge win! I get to sit & ask the real world questions that we all want to know and watch them knock out their fears & embrace their story...My energy & passion during the episodes is off the charts! MMTV has become my oxygen!

From the guests:

Denis Numera

Episode 4

denis@yesplace.org

Dave Daley, the Monster Motivator, does a great job with his Monster Motivator TV show. I've seen him bring out the best information from business owners who are on the show. He has a way of making people feel at ease, not only the guest, but also people who watch the show. If you want to get to know what is inside the head of a successful business owner, then this is the TV show you want to watch.
- Denis Numera , The Yes Place

Lori McMacken aka Lori Mac

Episode 10

lorimac7777@gmail.com

Dave Daley The Monster Motivator, Arghhhh! Interviewed me on MMTV and I was so thrilled to be his 10th guest. He came to my home where I felt comfortable and created an atmosphere where it was easy for me to open up about my life's journey. Dave's personal message is about breaking thru fear barriers and living your peak potential. His message is in alignment with my life experiences. Dave asked me the right questions, which took the viewer on a journey of expansion. Dave was interested and wanted to know where my journey in life began, he wanted to know my WHY and what drove my career. He wanted to find out what paradigms changed my life and HOW. Dave has the wisdom to know that the twist and turns in life, give's each individual inspiration to make break throughs that assist in manifesting one's biggest dreams. Dave quotes that personal success is... "The same recipe but different ingredients for each person". He was sincerely interested in hearing what changed my mindset what helped me to break through in order to express my talent in the world as a Radio City Rockette and a Real Estate Investor. Dave asked the right questions to seed the story his viewers were waiting to hear. The Monster Motivator looks like a pit bull but acts like a big kitten at heart. Hands down my favorite part of the Monster Motivator is his growl! And it doesn't sound like a purr...... Arghhhhh!

-Lori McMacken

Anthony Steel & Forrest Follen

Episode 19

ANTHONYSTEEL1981@yahoo.com

Website: http://wayoflifebootcamp.com/

Facebook:
https://www.facebook.com/thewayoflifebootcamp/?fref=ts

My experience with Dave Daley was amazing on his motivational talk show it felt really good to be able to get the opportunity to talk about who I am and what my purposes here on this earth the questions that he asked really spurned me towards saying the exact things that were going to touch the people in a major way especially them out to people that are listening these on a social network and how he repurposes it to YouTube and other other social networksI hope that I have another opportunity to be on Dave showed to be able to create impact that we created on our last show
- Anthony Steel

Our experience for MMTV was a blast! The LIVE conversation was extremely well-led by Dave. He has a way with getting us to tell relevant stories that give value to the viewer and to us at the same time. We did it LIVE right there in our fitness facility, and it was done in a way that wasn't over-structured, so we were able to walk around and do a more intimate interview in the office, then go out and do "on-the-spot" interviews with clients and watch the action on the training floor. Our clients and staff loved it! From a media standpoint, getting the exposure was great, and I noticed it was launched over multiple channels so we appreciated the marketing buzz. Dave even gave the group some free coaching at the end! It was awesome! Way to over deliver!!
- Forrest Follen

Cyndi Lemke

Episode 31

cyndi@lemkesleverage.com

Website: www.lemkesleverage.com

Facebook: https://www.facebook.com/LemkesLeverage/

I heard Dave at an event and was immediately motivated to work harder for my new business, wanting to learn more about him and hear more of his messages I attended a couple more events and eventually met him; what an amazing impact he has had on me! Dave has engrained in me to think about accountability, what I allow to help or hinder my productivity. We all have an excuse for things not getting done or may have "one of those days'...I don't think Dave does, he is always working hard to make an impact on his goal and that is contagious, at the very least I think about everything I do and how it will or will not impact my goals.

I had the opportunity to be interviewed on MMTV and was a little apprehensive to get on LIVE, but Dave was so great by just having a conversation with me that I was able to answer his questions from the heart and let people learn about me and where I started. I have received such positive feedback about my episode and am now facing opportunities because people had the chance to learn about me and what I do.

The great thing about MMTV is that every week I get to watch an episode about someone else's story. These stories are relatable, inspiring and without a doubt I look forward to meeting these people through Dave's interview because he draws out the best of us by being real, raw and live!!! Thank you for all you do Dave!!

- All the best. Cyndi Lemke

Shelly Rufin

Episode 32

shelly@edfincashforcollege.com

Website: www.edfincashforcollege.com

Facebook:
https://www.facebook.com/EDFINCashforCollegeTemecula/

Monster Motivator TV allowed me to share my story about why I'm where I'm at today as an Expert College & Financial Aid Planner and to inspire others, single moms, business owners that there is no excuse for pursuing your dreams. The only one holding you back for accomplishing your god given talents is you. My interview with Dave Daley was an amazing high energy, no excuses interview talking about my humble beginnings growing up as a child where the importance of an education wasn't paramount, and never discussed in our family. As a young women in my 20's, I gravitated to education and it became my outlet to learn more. Now years later, I've completed my B.S. Management, Masters of Science in Human Services and Clinical Counseling and Neuroscience pursuing my PhD in Psychology Industrial Organization. Dave Daley MMTV interview was an amazing experience which allowed me to share my accomplishments as a professional, and the human side of being married for 28 years (multicultural marriage), three boys and inspire others you to can accomplish your dreams, goals aspirations in life. You're going to have to work hard, make many sacrifices and never lose sight of why your "Why". Three D's: Determination to never give up, Desire to follow your dreams, and Discipline to stay focused. Highly recommend Dave Daley!

- Shelly Rufin, Expert College & Financial Aid Planner, Author of "Making College DREAMS a Reality " and Speaker.

Janel Keas

Episode 33

janel@smurfmom.com

Website: http:// www.smurfmom.com

Being on Monster Motivator TV was an empowering experience for me. To be able to share my story and passion was uplifting in itself. But the realization that others were encouraged by what I had to say, that was like a super boost! With life having the kinds of ups and downs that shake many of us to our core, sometimes there remains the question of "Why?". But as I progress through this journey that is my life, I have come to

realize that no matter what we encounter, as we share it and verbalize the feelings and lessons learned, those around us are encouraged to power on. This is why, as humans, we were not intended to walk out journeys alone. This was the greatest impact on me in being interviewed by Dave on his show...MMTV is an opportunity to share with each other, derive strength from each other's stories. Literally a buffet of experiences to load up our sometimes empty plates with wisdom, inspiration and the courage to face our fears head on. It's been said that not all things faced can be changed. But nothing changes until faced. MMTV is an opportunity and experience that makes that possible, on so many different levels. Thank you, Dave, for the chance to be part of the movement that is MMTV. The opportunity you give others to share is life altering. Rock on!
- Janel Keas

Suzanne Hamilton-Powers aka SuzyQ

Episode 34

Team4Lifesdca@gmail.com

Website: http://powers.pruvitnow.com

My First Exposure To Monster Motivator TV was via San Diego Networking and Events on Social Media.

I Would Ck The Posts Regularly To Keep Up With Events Locally. I Began Likely Some Of Dave's Motivational Posts and Then Making Comments & Reposting To My FB Page To Motiviate and Inspire Others. Dave & I Communicated back and Forth on the comments & Thus The Following Began. One day I said Outloud To My Spouse, "I Would Like To Connect With Dave From MMTV.

I Think It Would Help Me Get The Word Out About KetoOS!"
Literally Within 10 min. Dave Messaged Me To Invite Me For An
Interview! WOW! Brilliant Minds DO THINK ALIKE!!

Right Away I Was Able To Schedule My Interview! Dave Has A
Way To Put You At Ease. He Has The Knack To Ask The Right
Questions and Prompt Thought Process To Bring Up Memories
And Allow Space To Share "RAW & REAL"

I Nervously Began To Share About My Childhood Forward and
Throughout My Sports And School Adventures. Giving the
Viewers Insight Into ME.

We Had A BLAST! After The Interview, I Had 20+ hits & inquiries
on My FB! Still Have On Going Friend Requests Coming In Daily!

I am Looking Forward To My Follow Up Interview, Here In The
Near Future!

I Have Also Been Connecting Dave With Some Amazing People
To Interview & Motivate on MONSTER MOTIVATOR TV!!

- Suzanne Hamilton-Powers aka #SuzyQPowers

- TEAM 4 LIFE

- Independent Promoter Prüvit KetoOS

Will Boudrow & VIP Guest Sandy

Episode 35

weboudrow@yahoo.com

Website: http://www.sweven.paycation.com

I have known Dave Daley for a little over a year. He only knew a portion of my history, yet was interested in what made me who I am. He asked me to be on his show and provide my story to the public. At first, I was hesitant, due to the nature of my story. I do not like talking about what I have been through. He told me that I needed to tell my story, only because someone may be able to benefit from it. That caused me to rethink the way I look at what I have been through. It completely changed how I approach talking to people about the details of my experiences.

The interview was pretty awesome! I was extremely excited to sit with Dave and talk. He made the interview feel like it was more of a conversation than an interview. I enjoyed the overall experience.

- Will Bourdrow

Brittany-Rose Tribulski

Episode 36

themvrose@yahoo.com

Website: www.lakesidepest.com

Facebook: https://www.facebook.com/Lakeside-Pest-Control-675634415827843/?fref=ts

MMTV was a great experience! Dave Daley really connected with me and connects well with an audience. Dave came to me and we made it happen. If you want to be motivated and if you want to succeed, listen up to the Goodness that Dave brings to the world. Get pumped up for your life! Thank you Dave for the great experience and I suggest we do another interview in a year from now to show the unfolding of success! Thank MMTV! Swimming in the Goodness by Aaron Christopher Kirkeby

Montser Motivator was an inspiring experience. Watching the show helped me hear other people's story and get to know them and their businesses on a deeper level.

When I was asked to participate I wasn't sure what I could offer to others. As I told my story I began to remember how far I have come and how all my successes and setbacks had added to my life.

As people interacted with us online, it became a really fun experience and I started connecting with new people in my community that related to my story. Even my sister called me to discuss everything she learned and how she changed aspects of her business based on some topics Dave Daley and I discussed.

Overall it was a blast! I am better connected to those around me and still get emails from people that watched the episode to tell me how I inspired them. What a shock!

- Brittany Tribulski

Larry Lewis Jr.

Episode 3 & 37

musclemeditationfitness@gmail.com

Website: www.musclemeditationfitness.com

Facebook: https://www.facebook.com/larrylewisjr

Dave's the best at bringing out the best of you right there as you are it's the real you present. Dave's energy and insightful questions had me putting out golden nuggets didn't know I had in me! Monster Motivator has been a blessing forcing me to look at myself and how bad I want it I am happy to say I now have it! Thank you Dave The Monster Motivator for helping me to crush my fear barriers!

- Larry Lewis Jr

Abigail Robinson

Episode 38

abigailrpes@gmail.com

Website: www.acceleratecenter.com

Facebook: https://www.facebook.com/acceleratecenter

Before I went on Monster Motivator TV, I was fearful about being online; because as a side effect of a stroke that I had suffered earlier this year, I still occasionally stutter and forget my train of thought... My biggest fear was how I was going to remember all of the questions that I would be asked and then having to paraphrase my answers without stuttering and forgetting what I was talking about. However to my great surprise, Dave's interview was unlike any other I had experienced! His interview was unscripted, real, raw, and unfiltered. I was at ease during the interview and because of him I conquered one of the fears that had been weighing me down. I loved the opportunity to share my story in the hopes that it might help inspire someone.

After the interview, I developed a new sense of self confidence and I have made many new contacts and connections.

MMTV adds intrinsic and extrinsic value to others as it is a positive, unique, and a free way for entrepreneurs to find one another and also acts as a conduit for linking an entire

160

community of resources. What's best is that because of this, entrepreneurs can collaborate with one another, grow and thrive to become out better selves. Thank you Dave Daley, and thank you MMTV for the opportunity to break my fear barriers!

- Abigail Robinson

Rob Cando

Episode 39

candocomputerrepair@gmail.com

Website: http://www. candocomputerrepair.com

Facebook: www.facebook.com/candocomputerrepair

Not only is Monster motivator TV an awesome program but it's life-changing.

It changed my life by allowing me to observe myself to see where I'm going, where I am now and how far I came in life. I love myself more, I love God more and I believe him more because of the gift I got sent in the name of Dave Daley!

Dave you're an awesome man! I support you and Monster Motivator TV 100%. I love you bro!
- Rob Cando

Julia Rogoff

Episode 41

gobnnas.julia@yahoo.com

Facebook: www.facebook.com/cultivatinginclusion

Being on MMTV was quite eye opening. I am more of a doer then a talker so having to share my experiences at the interview was challenging. I thought Dave asked insightful questions that gave us the opportunity to have a great conversation. I was surprised at how much we had in common. Many people don't look at founders of non profits and see a business person but Dave was able to really drive that point home. I would recommend being on MMTV to anyone who has a story to tell, and really isn't that all of us!

-    Julia Rogoff

April Vidal

Episode 42

APRILVIDAL1@GMAIL.COM

Facebook: www.facebook.com/missaprilsdance

Dave Daley is a pure genius when it comes to keeping integrity of one's self whether starting a business, running a business, or even having to let go of a business.
When asked to be a guest on DDMM, I was not only excited but enthusiastic about supporting someone who supports so many others. His smile is infectious, his message is easily digested and he has definitely made me realize who the Tommy's of my life are.
We all need that push, that drive, that motivation to continue on setting goals and acheiviing them. Dave has hit that theory right on the head by asking so many to share their personal stories to share with others. In business we need to realize as in life itself, we were all made up differently, but we all have the same tools to succeed, fail, and succeed over and over again.

Dave's DDMM allows every viewer to listen, over and over again to ways to self motivate and accomplish those dreams we bury deep inside of ourselves due to fear of failure. May this book of his bring you peace of mind that you can succeed , will succeed, and share by helping others succeed.
Be Yourself.
- April. J. Vidal, Miss April's Dance

Avid fan and follower of Monster Motivator TV – Hasn't missed one episode!!

Ever so true. I fell into that trash can when my Robert passed away. Three decades had passed as that's how long we were together and I thought I had been left alone in a strange new world. I was the perfect target as I had allowed myself (at the time without knowing) to become a victim. I lost virtually everything...and I realized I had become spiritually defunct. That's when I got mad. But instead of acting out my anger, I prayed my head off. I started using every issue as a learning experience. Thank God and my parents had bright kids, because learn I did...and fast & furious. I love my life, through all its thorns and flowers. But now I have pity on those who even think I'm a mark. It's called I will do whatever it takes to defend my life, time and my kindness. I just love your posts. Puts me back to where I was and where I am now. Thank you Dave Daley for all you do, not just for me but for those who choose to get as much out of your posts as you put into them. Sincerest blessings.
Deborah Anderson

In 2013, after 14 years of marriage, I found myself on my own...a single mom of 3. I had been a stay at home mom all those years so I faced a very uncertain future with no job skills in a small town with little hope for the future. I floundered and searched for answers and support but nothing seemed to work for me. In the early summer of 2015, I was introduced to Dave Daley through a mutual friend. I had no idea what I was in store for. We struck up a personal friendship and I found that I could turn to Dave for sage wisdom and life advice that made sense to me. At the time, I had no idea what he did for a living and suggested he become a motivational speaker!!

Dave Daley, The Monster Motivator is extraordinary. I'm glad that so many people get to be a part of his dream. His live program on Monster Motivator TV now enables him to reach countless people who just need a light at the end of their tunnel. Dave asks the right questions of his guests, getting them to open up and share personal experiences that. no matter who you are, will touch a cord and resonate with everyone. What I truly appreciate about Dave is that when he asks a question, whether its about someone's business or how they are feeling, he really wants to know. He's a genuine spirit and really cares. His guests are fun and informative and share invaluable insights into life and business that no one should miss.

In my humble opinion, Dave Daley is one of the best people I know.

- Teri Williamson, Benson, Arizona

I look forward to watching Dave Daley Monster Motivator's interviews of local business, charities, and community members who make a difference in the Temecula Valley. In each episode, I learn about the business owner being interviewed as well as the challenges they've overcome both personally and professionally. Feeling connected in this way encourages me to seek them out for services above all others. Additionally, Dave Daley's energy is contagious. His no-nonsense, no excuses style puts him in a category of motivational greats like Grant Cardone and Gary Vaynerchuk.

Cheers to your continued success... Ahhhhh

Trish Duarte

42210 Roick Drive Suite 11
Temecula, Ca 92590
P: 951-506-6100 Option 2 **F:** (951) 225-1129
E: temecula@maidpro.com - **W:** www.maidpro.com/temecula
Facebook: www.facebook.com/ temeculamaidpro
Twitter: twitter.com/maidpro

I was surrounded by people that didn't understand me or what I offered so I went to where people appreciated my resources...1 year later I have been the vehicle for many women to connect & grow through networking together at meet ups & events I created and host 100 miles from where I live...I am loving this interview!!!!!

Lisa Harris McLean

Total Inspiration!!!

Lori Curran

Made in the USA
San Bernardino, CA
31 August 2016